P9-DTA-795

"Most people think about insurance after the fact—when they're forced to confront the reality of too little insurance or the wrong coverage. **Read this book and make the necessary changes in your insurance now. You'll save money and purchase peace of mind.**"

> TERRY SAVAGE
> Author of *Terry Savage's New Money Strategies for the '90s*

"**Bamford has done it!** She has taken the normally confusing explanations of over-, under-, and uninsured and explained them in **simple and concise terms** for the consumer. Applying the concepts outlined in this book will **save money for every reader!**"

> ANDREW M. HUDICK, MS, CFP
> Fee-Only Financial Planning, L.C.
> Former President, National Association
> of Personal Financial Advisors

"I'm impressed! Bamford's book is **packed with gems to save you time, money, and aggravation.** She has **sound answers** to questions you should be asking about your insurance coverage. **I plan to give this book to my clients.**"

> DEENA KATZ, CFP
> Evensky, Brown, Katz & Levitt
> Former Chair, International Association
> of Financial Planners (Chicago Chapter)

SMARTER

Insurance
SOLUTIONS

Also available from
the Bloomberg Personal Bookshelf

A Commonsense Guide to Mutual Funds
by Mary Rowland

SMARTER
Insurance
SOLUTIONS

JANET BAMFORD

ILLUSTRATIONS BY WARD SCHUMAKER

Bloomberg Press

◆

PRINCETON

Bloomberg Press books are available for bulk purchases at special discounts for educational, business, or sales promotional use. Special editions or book excerpts can also be created to specifications. For information, please write: Special Markets Department, Bloomberg Press, 100 Business Park Drive, P.O. Box 888, Princeton, NJ 08542-0888 U.S.A.

Library of Congress Catalog Card Number 96-084216
ISBN 1-57660-003-3

Bloomberg Press books are printed on acid-free paper.

This publication is designed to provide accurate and authoritative information. It is sold with the understanding that the publisher is not engaged in rendering legal, accounting, investment-planning, or other professional services. If legal advice or other expert assistance is required, the services of a competent professional person should be sought.

First edition published 1996

1 3 5 7 9 10 8 6 4 2

Acquired and edited by Christine Miles

Book Design by Don Morris Design

To Peter and Gregory

— J . B .

ACKNOWLEDGMENTS

I WAS FORTUNATE IN WORKING on this project to have had the help of the talented staff of Bloomberg Press, most notably Christine Miles. I have been the lucky recipient of Chris's support and wise editorial insights for several years. Betsy Ungar left a trail of valuable suggestions as she traveled through the copy. Barbara Diez, who could no doubt effectively reorganize the Pentagon if she so wished, applied her considerable management skills to copy editing and coordinating the publication of this book. Don Morris and Josh Klenert designed this book to be a pleasure to look at, while Marcia Matrisciano miraculously turned dense tables into helpful illustrations. I am also indebted to Alice Huston, my resourceful research associate, who spent long hours on the telephone tracking down information, and to Lisa Nikulicz, for her painstaking fact-checking. Jared Kieling and Bill Inman have supported and helped shape the book from its earliest days, while both Kieling and John Crutcher are even now tirelessly working to bring it to the attention of potential readers.

I would also like to thank the three families, the Whartons, the Bittenbrings, and Brenda Rhodes, for graciously allowing us in to take a closer—and more public—look at their insurance dealings, as well as Janet Briaud, Diahann Lassus, and David Drucker, the astute financial planners who lent their expertise. I am also indebted to the many industry observers and experts, most of whom are mentioned within the text, who gave graciously of their time and wisdom while I was preparing this book.

And finally, I would like to thank my husband, David Coats, who lent encouragement and cheerfully did more than his share of tag-team parenting in the last year, and my beloved children, Peter and Gregory Coats, who learned to ask, "Are you working?" and quietly back out of my office before interrupting a phone conversation. If insurance is a tool for shielding loved ones from risk, they are the best reason for using such a tool.

INTRODUCTION

ET'S FACE IT. Buying insurance is no fun. You are forced to consider all sorts of disagreeable possibilities, like car accidents, fires, chronic illness, and death. When you apply for insurance, you are required to fill out applications that ask for the most intimate details of your life and perhaps ask you to prove your health, your income, or the worth of your home. Then you have to pay. Insurance costs plenty, and you don't have anything in particular to show for it—unless, heaven help you, calamity should actually hit.

So, the only thing less fun than buying insurance is not having it. Without insurance, you could lose all your financial assets—your home and your savings and investments—because of a fire or serious illness requiring prolonged medical care. Looking for an immediate, tangible

benefit from insurance? Here's one: it enables you to sleep more soundly at night.

In most households insurance is a major expenditure. The insurance department of the Consumer Federation of America estimates that consumers in the United States spend about 16 percent of their annual incomes on insurance coverage. If you include what you or your employer pays for your health insurance, your total tab probably comes in third (after food and housing)

on your list of annual expenditures. I know
families that easily pay more to provide health
insurance for four than to feed four. All in all,
Americans pay about $180 billion a year in
insurance bills.

Surprised? If so, it's probably because your
insurance purchases are so fragmented. You may
buy an auto policy from one agent, a life-
insurance policy from another agent, and get
disability coverage in a group policy available
through your employer. Your homeowners
insurance or some mortgage life insurance may
be lumped into your monthly mortgage payment.
It's easy to lose track of all the dollars, but when
they're added together, chances are they equal
a hefty chunk of your income.

This book is designed to help you clarify your
needs and to offer smarter solutions to insurance
buying. It simplifies the process of considering all
your needs as a whole and gives you telephone
numbers to call for more information. You'll find

over a hundred tips highlighting things you could overlook in a policy containing 10 pages of small type. I have included lots of stories from people on the front lines of insurance buying, trying to get you real-life news you can use. They tell you how to look at the overlaps and gaps in your combined insurance policies, guidance that can pay off by actually increasing your protection while saving you some money.

EVERY ONE OF US CAN use this kind of help. Consumers are notoriously bad insurance buyers. Few people aggressively shop for coverage, deferring to agents who may have vested interests in pushing one type of policy over another. A study published by the Insurance Research Council found that more than 50 percent of those surveyed either took an agent's recommendation or bought auto and homeowners insurance from the first company they contacted. This despite the fact that premiums for similar auto and

homeowners policies can vary tremendously—
by as much as 100 percent.

A few years ago, then–Texas Insurance
Commissioner Robert Hunter and his staff came
up with an automobile-insurance shopping guide
for Texas residents. As part of the promotional
effort, the department brought in a group of
people whose auto policies were coming up for
renewal, gave them each a copy of the guide,
access to a telephone, and an hour to see if they
could save money on their auto coverage by
shopping around. They did, and impressively.
"The average person saved $172 in an hour," says
Hunter. "How many people can make $100 for
an hour's work?"

Broadly speaking, all insurance works the same
way. You pay a fee, or premium, to the insurance
company, and it pays you a specific sum if certain
things happen. The insurance company's
actuaries, its statistical whiz kids, calculate the
likelihood of something happening, and your

premium varies according to those statistical possibilities. If you're 58 years old and have had triple-bypass heart surgery, you have a better chance of dying than a college athlete, so you pay more for life insurance. If you're a hormone-charged 19-year-old sports-car driver, statistics say you've got a better chance of being in a car accident than a 45-year-old with three kids, so your auto-insurance premiums are higher. And if you live 150 yards from the beach, you're more likely to see your house wash away in a storm, so your homeowners premiums are sky-high.

At some point your chances are deemed so bad that it may be tough to get insurance at any price. But often for auto, homeowners, and health insurance, state or federal government programs will enable you to get some kind of coverage, although it may come at a high cost.

Here are the basic questions any consumer should ask when buying insurance:

Do I need it? If you have a car, of course you need auto insurance. But the arguments for other types of insurance, such as life insurance, aren't so obvious. The fellow next door may need it while you don't. And some types of coverage nobody needs: trip insurance that will pay if you have bad weather on a vacation and contact-lens insurance are both examples of junk policies. Ask yourself, what dire financial consequences could I suffer if something happens? If you can't come up with an answer, skip the coverage.

Can I afford to pay for these losses? To get good value in your insurance policies, don't sweat the small stuff. Never insure yourself for an amount that you can afford to pay out of your savings; self-insuring is far more efficient than buying insurance for small losses. That is the principle behind taking large deductibles. Insurance premiums drop dramatically if you're willing to pay the first, say, $500 of your bills, because the insurer pays less, or perhaps nothing, out of its kitty.

What kind of policy should I buy? Auto and homeowners policies are fairly standard, although there are all types of special riders (or additions) to consider. Health-insurance and disability policies are more complicated. But they're all just a warm-up for life policies, which come in variation upon variation. Like a baroque fugue, some policies have themes that double back on one another. There's universal life insurance, variable life, and of course, universal variable life. Each policy has its own uses, risks, and rewards. You need to understand them all before you can shop intelligently.

From whom should I buy it? These days, you're not limited to the insurance agent who has an office on Main Street. There are also direct writers—companies that will sell you policies without using agents, over the telephone. Even discount brokers like Charles Schwab & Co. have gotten into the business lately, selling low-load life-insurance policies. Cutting out the middleman often allows them to offer lower rates. It seems clear that in the not-too-distant future, your local bank will offer insurance beyond the savings-bank life insurance that is available in a few states now. When you get a mortgage, it's conceivable that you'll be able to sign up for homeowners insurance on the spot.

Each of these different distribution methods has advantages and costs. Understanding them will allow you to decide which trade-offs to make.

How much should I pay? Just asking that question gets you off on the right foot. Prices for policies vary widely, and knowing that will give you the impetus to do a little comparison shopping. This book will provide you with some benchmark costs.

What's the reputation of the insurance company? You don't just want the lowest-cost insurance; you want the highest-quality insurance you can get at the lowest cost. Your insurance contract is only as good as the company behind it.

Think of the advertising slogans used by most of the major insurance companies, mottos like "You're in good hands," "Like a good neighbor," and "A piece of the rock." They are all crafted to sound sturdy and reassuring. That's because, in essence, what you're buying is a promise. A company has to be financially stable enough to pay off on its promises. You also want to buy insurance from a company that has a good reputation for settling claims and dealing well with its customers. Who needs a hassle collecting after living through a trauma?

THE NEXT SEVERAL YEARS promise to be unsettling ones for the insurance industry. The ranks of agents are shrinking as more and more insurance is sold through direct-market approaches. Consumers are becoming increasingly savvy, demanding lower agents' commissions and better service. At the same time, regulatory changes in many states mean that insurers' finances are under less scrutiny than they have been in the past few years. So individuals have to be more aware than ever of an insurance company's financial strength.

In all, there's never been a better time, or a more important one, to be a vigilant insurance consumer.

Auto
INSURANCE

Feeling Lost? Here's Help

UYING AUTO insurance isn't a "should I or shouldn't I?" decision. If you own a car, state laws require you to be financially responsible for any damage you do with it. Most states actually require you to have insurance; others have "financial responsibility" laws that make you liable. Even in those states, for all practical purposes insurance is the easiest way to guarantee that you can meet your obligations.

Assuming you want to remain a law-abiding citizen, the only questions are: What type of auto coverage should you buy? How much do you need? And how can you get the best deal?

Answering those questions can be complicated. Different states mandate different kinds of coverage, and you need to know not only what types of insurance to buy but also what discounts are available and what strategies you can use to

lower premiums. This chapter tries to clear some of the complications by giving money-saving pointers about liability, collision and comprehensive, and personal-injury protection.

But first things first. The most important thing to know about automobile insurance is that if you don't actively shop around, you may be missing some significant savings.

Americans spent an average of $650 per car on auto insurance in 1994, the most recent year for which statistics are available. That's not small change. And for many, the costs are much greater. Drivers in densely populated areas and high-insurance states, such as Connecticut, Hawaii, and New Jersey, pay premiums that average more than $1,000. Families with more than one car or with teenaged drivers, or drivers who commute long distances can easily spend $5,000 a year on insurance. In fact, if you own a car for more than a few years and live in a region where insurance rates are high, you may spend more insuring your vehicle than you did buying it.

Despite the large sums involved, though, remarkably few consumers actually shop for their auto insurance; most simply sign with the first company they get a quote from. A 1995 survey by the Insurance Research Council (IRC) found that 55 percent of the respondents either had agents choose for them or had decided on one company from the start of the process.

Even those who do research their alternatives usually stop after signing the contract. That may be too soon: an insurance company that is cheapest one year may not remain the best deal a few years down the road. Nevertheless, the 1995 IRC study showed that only 27 percent of drivers had changed their policies or made any inquiries about doing so in the past five years. Ideally, auto-insurance policies should be shopped for and reviewed every two or three years.

Comparison shopping can pay off in a big way. There are wide variations in how much different companies in the same region will charge the same consumer for the same coverage.

For instance, the California Dept. of Insurance's annual survey, which asks automobile-insurance companies to give rates for several hypothetical consumers, found that premiums vary by as much as 300 percent.

In the 1995 survey, insurers were asked to price a basic policy on a 1992 Toyota Camry and a 1994 Ford Explorer owned by a husband and wife, ages 45 and

43, living in Los Angeles. The pair were assumed to have one speeding ticket each on their records and a 17-year-old son who is an occasional operator. The results, shown below, illustrate the startling disparity among auto-insurance premiums.

Mercury General	$5,560
Liberty Mutual	$5,587
Inter-Insurance Exchange of AAA	$6,630
Viking/Talegen	$6,851
ITT/Hartford	$7,294
Safeco Insurance	$7,358
Fireman's Fund	$8,187
State Farm	$10,432
Allstate	$11,590
Unitrin/Financial Indemnity	$12,945
National General	$17,782

Moreover, one company may be relatively cheap for some policies and relatively expensive for others. In the California survey, Mercury General's quote was not the lowest for all hypothetical situations, nor was National General's the highest.

☞ **Cruise the whole auto-insurance market.**
Check with some of the larger carriers, like State Farm and Allstate, which together cover nearly one in five Americans. In addition, you can get quotes over the phone from direct-dial insurers such as GEICO (800-841-3000), USAA (800-531-8100), American Express Co. (800-535-2001), and 20th Century (in California and Arizona, 800-211-SAVE). Be aware that USAA sells auto primarily to military officers and their families.

You should also call one of the quote services. Long a boon to consumers shopping for term-life coverage, these services are beginning to blossom in the auto-insurance market as well. They'll give you several quotes over the phone, making it easier for you to compare policies. Con-

sumers Union (parent company of *Consumer Reports* magazine) offers an auto-insurance quote service for California,
Florida, New York, and Washington (800-807-8050).
Reports are $12 for the first vehicle and $8 for the second.
Insurance Information, Inc., which has been offering quotes
on life insurance for years, is developing an automobile-
insurance quote service. For information and prices, call
800-472-5800.

Progressive Insurance Corp. (which first became known
for its willingness to insure higher-risk drivers; see page 33)
runs a hot line at 800-AUTO-PRO (800-288-6776) that will
give you quotes on the company's own policies as well as on
those of up to three other insurers. The service is free, but
obviously Progressive hopes you'll decide to buy its policy.
The hot line is available in 45 states, excluding Massachusetts, New Jersey, North Dakota, South Carolina, Washington, D.C., and West Virginia.

☞ Call your state insurance department, or cruise the Internet.

Several states (see the "State-by-State Guide," page 218)
publish auto-insurance shopping guides that compare rates
within the state. The guide for your state can give you a general idea of which companies sell insurance in your area and
what rates they charge. Many states are also setting up
Web sites on the World Wide Web. The Insurance News Network (http://www.insure.com) offers consumer information
from several states; the Web site for the National Association of Insurance Commissioners (http://www.naic.org) can
give you information on how to reach your own state's
home page.

☞ Pool your business.

If you have more than one car, there is usually a discount for
insuring them all with one company. Some insurers will give
you a break if they cover both your car and your house.

COVERAGE: WHAT KINDS AND HOW MUCH DO YOU NEED?

IT HELPS TO THINK OF AN auto-insurance policy as several separate policies all rolled into one. Some types of coverage you might want and need; others might be unnecessary. Understanding the different components can help you decide what to buy and avoid paying for coverage you don't need. Some types of coverage will differ if you live in a no-fault state (more on page 25), but most basic necessary coverages apply to consumers in all states.

Liability coverage is what your state forces you to carry and what protects your assets in the event of a lawsuit. The two types pay for damage you do to other people and to property.

Bodily-injury liability covers the medical expenses and lost wages of any passengers in your car, as well as noneconomic losses, such as pain and suffering, if they are hurt or killed in an accident you caused. Bodily-injury liability also covers you for the occupants of the other car if you were at fault. In addition, it pays your legal costs if you're sued by anyone involved in the accident.

Property-damage liability covers injuries not to other people but to their possessions—their cars, a lamppost, whatever you might run into or over.

Together, the two types of liability coverage account for 40 to 50 percent of your total car-insurance premium. Bodily-injury and property-damage coverage is usually sold in a "split limit" format, which specifies the maximum amount the insurer will pay each person hurt in an accident and the total maximum per accident, as well as the total amount it will pay for property damage. For instance, a policy with 100/300/50 split limits would pay each injured passenger as much as $100,000, up to a ceiling of $300,000 in total payments per accident, and up to

$50,000 in property damage.

Liability coverage extends to another person driving your car with your permission. So if you lend your visiting brother your car and he causes an accident, your insurance covers him.

☞ **Don't leave yourself underinsured by buying the minimums required by law.**

How much liability insurance do you need? Theoretically, all you need is the legal minimum, which varies considerably from state to state. New York, for instance, mandates 25/50/10 coverage ($25,000/$50,000/$10,000), while Delaware requires only 15/30/10.

But remember—having only $30,000 of total bodily-injury liability coverage doesn't mean you can't be sued for more than $30,000 if you're in an accident. It just means that's all your insurance company will pay. That's why experts uniformly agree that the state minimums are much too low.

"People often don't understand what they're buying," says William Houston, a Denver-based insurance agent and CPCU (chartered property and casualty underwriter). "They're trying to clear the law so they can operate the vehicle, and they buy too low of a limit."

If you are sued, any judgment above your coverage has to come out of your savings or assets or, in some states, your future earnings. "People ask me what happens when they've maxed out on their coverage," says David Thompson, a Florida agent. "It's a bad situation, because once the auto policy has paid out the limits of liability, it's up to the client to figure out how the excess will be paid. I teach insurance at a local community college, and one of my students has a friend who is a professional jai alai player who has $50 a week garnished from his paycheck for an automobile accident claim."

Even in his fairly small insurance agency, Thompson says, he sees customers' auto-liability coverage "max out four or five times a year," always when the driver has insisted on taking only the legal minimum.

☞ **To protect your financial assets, make sure you have at least 100/300/50 of liability insurance. "Those are the minimums we recommend," says Houston.**
Opting for even greater bodily-injury liability coverage—say, up to a 250/500 limit—doesn't add much to your premium, perhaps an extra $150 a year, and increasingly is required by insurers before they'll add on an umbrella liability policy (more on that in "Homeowners Insurance," page 59).

COLLISION AND COMPREHENSIVE insurance covers damages to your own car. Collision pays to repair or replace your vehicle if you have an accident, whether or not you were at fault. If you were the innocent victim, though, your insurance company may try (or require you to try) to get the other guy's insurer to pay up.

Comprehensive covers the theft of your vehicle and damage from occurrences other than collisions. If a tree falls on your '96 Corvette, or it catches fire, or a windstorm tosses it about, comprehensive kicks in.

Neither collision nor comprehensive is required by the states. If you have a car loan or a lease, however, the lender will probably insist that you carry both types of coverage.

☞ **One rule of thumb experts use: if your insurance premium amounts to more than 10 percent of the value of the car, it's probably time to retire your collision and comprehensive coverage.**
Both collision and comprehensive are most useful when your car is fairly new and worth as much as it ever will be. Once it's more than about five to seven years old, think about dropping the coverage. If you have an accident and the car would cost more to fix than its blue-book value, the insurance company won't pay to replace or repair it. Instead, it will give you a check for the car's current value, minus whatever deductible you've selected. So as your car depreciates, the payment you would receive from the insurance

company shrinks, too. If you own an eight-year-old clunker with 120,000 miles on it, find out from your insurer how much you'd get if it were stolen or totaled.

Strictly speaking, you don't need collision or comprehensive even on a new car if you could replace it without financial hardship. Agent David Thompson tells of a client who declined collision coverage on his new Cadillac. "He told me that he was 71 years old, and if his car was wrecked today, he wouldn't like it, but he could come up with $25,000 to buy a new car without much trouble." That's an unusual consumer but one wisely willing to insure only for those losses he couldn't afford to pay for himself.

MEDICAL-PAYMENTS INSURANCE, generally offered in states without no-fault laws, pays doctor and hospital bills for all the people in your car, regardless of who is at fault. It also covers you for injuries you sustain while riding in someone else's car.

Medical-payments coverage usually isn't required by law, and your health insurance may already cover you and your family adequately. If so, you might want to skip the medical-payments portion of your policy and save yourself that part of your premium. One advantage of this coverage for drivers with their own health insurance is that nonfamily passengers can get reimbursed without actually having to file suit, as they'd have to, to collect under the bodily-injury portion of your policy. Then again, these passengers may have their own perfectly good health insurance.

If you have doubts about your health-insurance policy—if, for instance, it has a low lifetime maximum or you're unsure how far your coverage extends (is your college-age daughter who is taking a year off from school covered, for example?)—buy medical-payments insurance. Otherwise, find out how much you'd save by skipping it, and consider that option.

Personal-injury protection (PIP) covers much of the same ground, paying medical, hospital, and funeral expenses and some lost income, for you and your family, no matter who is at fault in the accident. It's usually required in no-fault states.

THE NO-FAULT SYSTEM

WHAT KIND OF AUTO INSURANCE you need depends in part on whether or not you live in a state that has instituted some type of no-fault auto insurance.

First, some brief background on no-fault insurance. Once upon a time, all states were "fault" states. In this type of system (sometimes called the "tort" system), the person who causes an accident—or, more accurately, his or her insurance company—pays for any injuries or damages he causes. Not surprisingly, this often leads to lengthy and expensive lawsuits, as opponents argue who is at fault, to what degree, and how much the nonculpable party should be awarded.

There are other big disadvantages to the "fault" system. If you are in an accident with someone who isn't insured or has too little insurance, you're out of luck. Unless the other motorist has pretty deep pockets and you can sue, you pay your own bills. (For uninsured-motorist protection, see page 27.)

This system was widely criticized for contributing to skyrocketing insurance premiums. The only people who truly benefit, it was said, are the lawyers involved, who typically earn contingency fees of one third the damage award.

Enter no-fault, a concept pioneered in 1966 by a University of Virginia law professor, Jeffrey O'Connell, and a Harvard law professor, Robert Keeton. In this system, currently in effect in 13 states, your own insurance pays for bodily injuries to you, your family, and your passengers, regardless of who's to blame. (No-fault doesn't address property damage, such as damage to your car, except in Michigan.)

The idea is to get the money more quickly to those who need it and to reduce the cost of insurance by lowering the number of lawsuits. The trade-off is that in no-fault states you're usually prohibited from suing except under certain conditions. Many no-fault states have also set limits on the dollar amount of reimbursements you can receive for medical and hospital expenses and for lost wages.

☞ **In the 13 states that now have some form of no-fault in place restricting the right to sue, accident victims can go after the negligent driver only under certain circumstances.**

To be eligible to sue, someone has to meet certain criteria. If they do, they can go to court for medical and other costs, and for pain and suffering as well.

Some states (Florida, Michigan, New Jersey, New York, and Pennsylvania) define serious cases by describing or listing them. This is called the "verbal threshold." Typically accidents that result in death, disfigurement, or severe impairment can be litigated.

Other states (Colorado, Hawaii, Kansas, Kentucky, Massachusetts, Minnesota, North Dakota, and Utah) use a monetary threshold: if your medical bills exceed a certain level, you can sue. Some states also take into account the number of days you've been disabled as a result of the accident. The monetary threshold varies from state to state. In Massachusetts, the threshold is a low $2,000; in Hawaii, it's $11,000.

A few states—Kentucky, New Jersey, and Pennsylvania—allow drivers signing up for a policy to choose between a verbal threshold limiting when they can sue and no restrictions on lawsuits. The no-restrictions policy comes with a higher auto-insurance premium.

No fault has had mixed success; in states where the monetary threshold is low it hasn't effectively curbed costs.

WHAT KINDS OF INSURANCE do you need in a no-fault state? Definitely liability coverage, since you can be sued if you're at fault in a serious accident. If you have

a car that's worth the coverage, you should get collision and comprehensive (no-fault almost never concerns itself with the damage done to your car).

And in no-fault states, you will be required to buy
personal-injury protection, which will pay medical,
hospital, and funeral expenses, as well as some lost
income, for you and your family and your passengers,
no matter who is at fault in an accident.

☞ Get uninsured-motorist coverage to protect your-self from scofflaws.

A survey done by the Insurance Research Council estimated
that 1 in 10 households with cars have uninsured vehicles.
Other experts put the numbers even higher, speculating
that more than 20 percent of the cars on the road are uninsured. Precise measurements are difficult, since few people
want to admit to driving without insurance. But clearly,
plenty of them are out there inflicting plenty of damage. A
1989 study found that 13 percent of all auto accidents are
caused by hit-and-run or uninsured drivers.

Those people are breaking the law and are subject to
penalties ranging from a fine to jail time if they are caught.
Of course, if you're unlucky enough to be hit and injured by
an uninsured motorist, it won't much matter to you that the
other guy is going to jail.

Remember, your liability insurance is to protect your
assets if you're sued and found to be at fault, not if somebody hits you. Even in a no-fault state, it can be a problem to
recover damages above and beyond the threshold in your
state if you collide with an uninsured motorist. You could
always sue the other driver, but it might be difficult to collect damages from someone who didn't have enough to buy
his own insurance coverage.

Underinsured drivers—those who obey the law by carrying only as much insurance as the state requires—also pose
a problem. If one of these collides with you and puts you in
the hospital, the mandated minimum bodily-injury coverage can evaporate in a few days.

This is where your uninsured- and underinsured-motorist insurance comes in. It pays medical expenses (as well as for noneconomic losses, such as pain and suffering), both for you and for passengers, and is well worth the cost. Many states even make it mandatory. It makes sense to buy uninsured- and underinsured-motorist protection in the same limits as you buy for coverage on your own auto: 100/300/50.

👉 **Choose the highest deductible you can afford for collision and comprehensive.**

The deductible is the amount you have to pay out of pocket before the insurance company will reimburse you for anything. You have to choose deductibles for both collision and comprehensive coverage, and you can choose different deductibles for each. Bigger is better: increasing your auto deductible from $200 to $500 could reduce your cost by 15 to 30 percent.

"The most common mistake we see people make is they don't buy high enough liability limits in auto, and then they'll turn right around and buy collision with a $50 or $100 deductible," says agent William Houston. "We like to use a deductible of $250 or $500 and, with the savings, make sure there are high enough liability limits."

Here's a suggestion for the extra cash you put in your pocket by taking a higher deductible: use it to self-insure for future out-of-pocket payments. That's what Robert Hunter, former state insurance commissioner of Texas, does. Each year for the past several years, he has calculated what he's saved on his premium by raising his deductible to the highest limit allowed by his insurance company, which is currently $1,000. Then he has deposited this amount in a savings account.

"It's my own casualty fund," he says. "I've done it for both auto and homeowners, and over the years I've come out ahead. I've paid two auto claims to myself and one homeowners, and I didn't even ask for photos when I paid my claim. I believe I have about $3,200 in that account currently."

👉 **Forget buying extra insurance when you are rent-ing a car—unless you are overseas.**

The liability and collision and comprehensive portions of your own car-insurance policy will cover a rental, and if you

WHAT A DIFFERENCE A DEDUCTIBLE MAKES

Below is a graphic demonstration of why you should opt for higher deductibles on your auto policy. It's a premium quote on a hypothetical couple living in Houston, Texas. John Doe, age 40, and his wife, Jane, age 38, have two cars and clean driving records. They drive a 1993 Ford Taurus and a 1994 Dodge Caravan and travel 10 miles and 20 miles, respectively, each way to work.

COVERAGE	$100 DEDUCTIBLE	$500 DEDUCTIBLE
Bodily-Injury Liability $100,000/$300,000	$386	$386
Comprehensive	172	93
Property-Damage Liability/$50,000	108	108
Collision	198	125
Total 6-Month Policy Premium	$864	$712

By increasing the deductibles on the collision and comprehensive portions of their policy from $100 to $500, the Does save $152 every six months, or more than $300 each year. At that rate, if they go two years without an accident, they're ahead even if they end up paying out the larger deductible at some point.

pay for the car with plastic, most credit-card companies provide collision coverage. The exception: if you're renting overseas, you're not covered by your own insurance policy.

👉 Don't bother with miscellaneous coverage.

Insurers offer a grab bag of other insurance services, including rental-car reimbursement and towing and labor insurance. Rental reimbursement usually provides only about $15
a day while your car is being repaired. If you can do without
a car for a couple of days, can borrow one, or can afford to
rent one yourself, this coverage doesn't make sense. As for
towing insurance, it's redundant if you belong to an auto
club. Even if you don't, an insurer typically reimburses you
only $25 to $75 of any towing bill. That's an amount you can
afford to pay yourself.

HOW YOUR POLICY IS PRICED

YOUR AUTO-INSURANCE PREMIUM is affected by several
factors. Some of them you can change, others you're
stuck with. For example, where you live is an issue. If
you live in the middle of a big city, you're more likely
to collide with another car or have your car stolen than
if you live in a rural area. So your rates are higher. On
the other hand, living close to where you work cuts
your insurance rates: you're on the road each day for
fewer miles and have a decreased chance of ending up
in one of those rush-hour pileups you hear about on
the traffic reports. For the same reason, retired people often pay less: they don't drive as much.

Your age and the ages of the other drivers in your
household also matter. When Maurice Chevalier sang
"I'm Glad I'm Not Young Anymore" in *Gigi*, he could
have been referring to his auto-insurance premiums.
Drivers under age 25 have a much higher accident
rate than older drivers, and their insurance bills
reflect the fact dramatically.

When I asked one insurance agent what would happen to my premiums when my two sons reached dri-

ving age, he replied, only partly in jest, "You need to run down to the U-Haul truck dealership, rent a big truck, and bring me a big box of money."

In contrast, if you're a senior citizen, you may qualify for a 10 to 20 percent discount, based on the fact that many older people don't drive as many miles a year as younger ones and are cautious drivers. Different companies make this discount available at different ages—anywhere from 50 to 65. But the senior years aren't all golden. Drivers older than 75 have a fatal-accident rate comparable to that of drivers aged 20 to 24. Consequently, many companies refuse to renew the policies of older customers after their 75th birthday or after they've had an accident. The American Association of Retired Persons (AARP) has an insurance program for older drivers. For information, call 202-434-2277.

Gender is another consideration. If you're a young man, you'll pay more for insurance than a woman of comparable age and driving record will. Young male drivers have more accidents, possibly because they spend more time behind the wheel than women. But accident rates among young women have risen significantly in the past five years, and their auto-insurance rates are sure to follow. Premium gender differences tend to level out as you age: a single male, age 45, typically pays the same as a single female, age 45.

Are married people more stable and cautious? Or are they just not as likely to be driving home from a date at 2 A.M. on a Saturday night after having had a few drinks? Married drivers between the ages of 25 and 50 get a normal adult rate. Many companies make single people wait until age 30 to qualify for that rate.

There's not much you can do about your age and sex, and you're probably not going to change where you live or your marital status to cut your car-insurance costs. Some factors, though, you can and should influence.

When you're shopping for a new car, keep in mind that what you drive affects your premiums. Rates on an economy car will be lower than on a luxury model, since an inexpensive car costs less to replace. Beyond that, big and boring tends to be cheaper than small and sporty. Insurers cringe at terms like *turbo-charged*. According to statistics from the Highway Loss Data Institute, the safest cars are big four-door models, station wagons, passenger vans, and those equipped with air bags and other passive-restraint equipment. (For a comparison of the highest- and lowest-cost cars to insure in their classes, see "Can You Afford to Insure It?" on the following page.)

Car-theft rates matter, too. The institute regularly publishes listings of the cars that are stolen most frequently. In its most recent survey, published in fall 1995, it found that the Ford Mustang, Mercedes 5-class series, Acura Legend, and Honda Prelude two-door were among cars thieves' favorite prey.

Another pricing variable you have control over is your driving record. Someone with a tarnished record is termed a "standard-risk driver" or, more seriously, a "substandard risk" and will typically pay 20 percent more than "preferred-risk drivers," who have clean records. So keep an eye on your speedometer.

A bad driving record can haunt you for a long time. Insurers will usually look at your record for the past three years; some will reach back as far as seven years, and others will ask on your application if you've had any major violations in the past 10 years. Traffic violations are not good, an accident in which you were at fault is bad, and a conviction for drunk driving is enough to make many companies refuse even to consider you. One reason many insurers have moved to six-month policies (renewed twice a year instead of once) is to have more opportunities to refuse to renew insurance for drivers who've piled up motor-vehicle violations.

Say you've had a clean driving record for years but then get a couple of speeding tickets within a few months. The next thing you know, you receive a notice that your insurer isn't renewing your policy when it expires. "Can it do this?" you ask. Yep, it can.

What an insurance company usually can't do is cancel your policy in the middle of a paid period. States generally allow that only if you don't pay a premium, if your driver's license is revoked or suspended, or if you made a significant misstatement on the policy application—for instance, if you forgot to mention that you have triplet 19-year-old sons who are driving your cars.

☞ **If you have a bad driving record, don't give up on finding insurance outside your state's high-risk pool.**
An estimated 8 million drivers in this country have trouble getting auto insurance. Luckily, some companies are willing to take a chance on high-risk clients, most notably, Progressive Insurance Corp., in Mayfield Village, Ohio. Call 800-288-6776 for a quote.

If that doesn't work, you will have to contact your state insurance department. Since states require you to be insured, they also mandate an insurance pool or some facility that must provide coverage to all applicants. These may be called joint underwriting associations, state-run pools, reinsurance companies, or assigned-risk pools. Whatever the name, their rates may be as much as 50 percent higher than those for normal policies.

☞ **Blots on your credit record—even temporary ones—can affect your chances of getting car insurance.**
Insurance companies say their statistics show a correlation between credit problems and claims filed. What's the connection? Maybe people with bad credit records have an incentive to file padded or fraudulent claims, or maybe they live in areas where their cars are more likely to sustain damage. Critics say credit-based denials discriminate against

CAN YOU AFFORD TO INSURE IT?

When you're looking for a new car, it pays to check with insurers to find out how much it will cost to insure it. That spirited sports car of your dreams can become a nightmare when you buy insurance. Some companies flatly refuse to write policies for high-priced sports cars like Porsches. Those that do offer coverage charge handsomely for it.

There are a couple of reasons for this. Not surprisingly, insurers assume that the buyers of high-performance vehicles are more likely to speed or drive dangerously. Those cars also tend to be more expensive to fix when damaged, and some perennially show up on the lists of the most-often stolen vehicles.

LOWEST	HIGHEST
Luxury	
$8,415	$19,888
Lincoln Town Car Signature	**Mercedes-Benz SL600/SL500 Roadster**
Base Sport	
$11,089	$16,770
Mazda MX-5 Miata	**Ford Mustang Cobra**
Sport	
$9,876	$19,888
Dodge Stealth	**Acura NSX**
Subcompact/Compact Wagon	
$7,061	$8,371
Saturn SW1	**Honda Accord EX**
Midsize/Large Wagon	
$7,061	$9,238
Oldsmobile Cutlass Ciera SL Cruiser and Ford Taurus GL	**Volkswagen Passat GLX**

At the other end of the spectrum, the cheapest cars to insure are larger (affording more passenger safety), loaded with features like air bags and impact-resistant bumpers, and not as alluring to car thieves.

The table below shows which autos have been cheapest and which most expensive in their class to insure over five years. Figures assume an average driver with a good record, living in a suburban area, putting about 14,000 miles a year on the odometer. They were compiled by IntelliChoice, a research firm that studies auto ownership and operating costs and publishes *The Complete Car Cost Guide.*

LOWEST	HIGHEST
Subcompact	
$7,364	$13,337
Suzuki Esteem GL 4-door	**Honda Prelude VTEC**
Compact	
$6,922	$9,583
Saturn SL and	**Audi A4 Quattro 4WD**
Hyundai Accent	
Midsize	
$6,922	$9,556
Olds Cutlass Ciera SL Series I	**Ford Taurus SHO**
Large	
$7,093	$8,892
Chevrolet Caprice Classic	**Toyota Avalon XLS**
Special Value SB	
Near Luxury	
$7,720	$14,103
Olds Ninety-Eight Regency	**BMW 328iC 2-door**
Elite Series I	

low-income drivers. Companies that use credit as a screen
include industry giant Allstate. If you think you've been
unfairly discriminated against on this count, call your state
insurance department.

☞ **Make sure you've asked for all the discounts
you're entitled to. Among the points you could receive
credit for:**

◆ **Antitheft devices:** Burglar alarms, disabling devices,
or hood locks can reduce the cost of the comprehensive
portion of your policy by 5 to 15 percent. These discounts
may be mandated by your state.

◆ **Carpools:** The theory here is that if you're carpooling,
you're driving less, reducing the chance you'll be in an
accident. Discounts can be in the 10 percent range.

◆ **Driver education:** A 5 to 15 percent discount is sometimes available to drivers who have taken a defensive-driving course or had driver training.

◆ **Good student:** If your driving-age son or daughter gets
good grades, don't hesitate to brag to your insurer about
it. Some companies offer discounts of 10 to 25 percent for
kids with grade averages of B (3.0) or better.

◆ **Out-of-town student:** If your child is attending college more than 100 miles from home, you can shave that
dreaded "young-driver premium" that is tacked onto your
family policy—provided, of course, he or she doesn't have
a covered car at school. The discount is usually about 10
to 15 percent.

◆ **Safety equipment:** Air bags can qualify you for a 20 to
50 percent discount on the medical and personal-injury
parts of your coverage. Factory-installed automatic safety belts can save you 10 to 30 percent on the same coverage. A couple of insurers give a discount on the collision
portion of your premium for factory-installed daytime
running lights. Fewer insurers, though, are offering discounts on antilock brakes.

INQUIRE ABOUT DISCOUNTS

	COMPANY A	COMPANY B	COMPANY C
$500 deductible			
$1,000 deductible			
More than 1 car			
No accidents in 3 years			
No moving violations in 3 years			
Drivers over 50 years of age			
Driver-training course			
Antitheft device			
Low annual mileage			
Automatic seat belt			
Air bag			
Antilock brakes			
Good grades for students			
Auto and homeowners coverage with the same company			
College students away from home without a car			
Other categories:			

SOURCE: INSURANCE INFORMATION INSTITUTE

☞ **If changes in your situation might entitle you to a rate cut—if you switch jobs and work closer to home, for instance—tell your insurer.**
Many companies ask policyholders to complete questionnaires once or twice a year to get updated information on how much driving they do and how many drivers are in their households.

☞ **Don't be tempted to shade the truth, either on an update or on your original application.**
You can bet that any insurer hit with a big claim will scrutinize your application carefully. If it can prove a deliberate misstatement, it can try to deny coverage. In addition, in some states you can be fined for "rate evasion" if you lie on your insurance application. Besides, insurers have access to your state's motor-vehicle records, which list any speeding tickets or moving violations you've earned. Also, CLUE (Comprehensive Loss Underwriting Exchange), a reporting agency, will tell companies and agents what claims you've filed recently and what licensed drivers live at your address.

WHEN YOU'RE IN AN ACCIDENT

STAY CALM AND FOLLOW these steps:

Contact the police immediately (they'll get the rescue squad, if necessary), and tend to any injured. Keep victims warm, and shield them from further injury, but don't try to move them.

Don't leave the scene of the accident. That's an imperative. However, insurers and authorities will generally give you some leeway if you can establish that you left in good faith and had reason to worry that you would have been in greater danger if you had stopped. This is a consideration, given the recent reports of carjackings, in which the thieves sideswipe a vehicle and then steal it when the driver pulls over. If you're in an accident and feel uncomfortable about stopping where you are—in a remote or poorly lit area, for instance—drive immediately to the nearest police station or to a safe location to report the incident.

Exchange information with the other parties in the accident: names, addresses, phone numbers, insurance companies and policy numbers, and make and model of car. (However, there's no need to tell anyone exactly what the limits of your coverage are; assuring them that you are insured is enough.) Do this before you leave the accident scene. Make careful notes about the accident, and if you have a camera handy, take photos.

Cooperate fully with the police, but stick to the facts. Don't jump to any conclusions or admit guilt. Find out how to get a copy of the police report and whether there will be a ticket issued to either driver.

Contact your insurer as soon as possible, ideally within 24 hours. Get damage estimates, and have your car inspected by the insurance adjuster. Some companies have drive-through claims centers, and some are beginning to experiment with networks of repair shops that will fix cars for set prices in return for the increased volume that an insurer can provide. These "preferred provider" arrangements for autos may well become as widespread as those in health care.

Keep careful records. Did you miss a paycheck because of an accident? You may be entitled to compensation. Are you unhappy with the insurance adjuster's estimate? Keep track of independent repair estimates. You may need them to prove you're entitled to a larger check.

☞ **File only your biggest claims and for fender benders involving another occupied car.**
Insurance companies often raise rates after settling claims.

The amount of the increase varies with the insurer. State Farm, for example, will add about 10 percent to three years of premiums if you file a "chargeable claim" (for an accident that's your fault) that costs the company more than $200. Other firms impose a larger penalty. Some companies, however, will allow you one accident claim without assessing a surcharge if you've been with them three to five years or more and have a clean driving record.

One benefit of a high deductible is that it can prevent you from filing small claims that will end up costing you more than you receive. "A string of little claims indicates claims consciousness," says William Houston, the Denver agent. "A couple of windshields, broken hubcaps—and a carrier might decide to get rid of you. They see you putting in claims for a new aerial and think, 'We're maintaining this guy's car. No matter what we collect in premiums, this guy is going to get it back, and we're left with the liability exposure.' We try to talk a client out of making lots of small claims."

If you cause an accident and pay for damages yourself instead of filing a claim, can you save money? Yes, but you're running a big risk. If the other driver sues you months later, your insurer can refuse to pay legal expenses because you failed to report the incident. Reporting it will not result in increased premiums if you pay for the damages instead of your insurer.

"If a client hits an occupied vehicle, I don't give them a choice. I report it to the company," says one agent. "Because if I don't and somebody claims a neck pain a few weeks later, I'm in trouble. But I had a client call last week and tell me they were backing out of their driveway and they hit somebody's car. If nobody was in the car, you might want to think about making an economic decision. You might have to pay $700 to fix their car, but if you put in a claim, your rates will go up $1,200 over the next three years."

☞ **Pick your insurer based on reports about its service as well as price.**

The last thing you need after an accident is an insurer who delays paying your claim or is hard to deal with. Unfortunately, service in the auto-insurance field has been woefully understudied. *Consumer Reports* magazine periodically publishes the results of a survey asking readers about the service provided by their insurers and ranks the companies accordingly. The most recent survey was published in October 1995 and is available in most public libraries.

CHAPTER

Homeowners
INSURANCE

Can You Replace Your Place?

I F YOU'RE LIKE MOST of us, your home represents the single largest investment you'll ever make, and homeowners insurance protects it. Home destruction from hurricanes and brush fires makes the headlines, but insurance also covers more ordinary occurrences: a hailstorm, a kitchen fire, or a burglary, for example. It shields your personal property and provides you with liability insurance in case someone slips on your sidewalk or is bitten by your dog.

Homeowners insurance used to be pretty much of a no-brainer. Getting coverage was a matter of placing a quick call. It was fairly cheap, and application forms and appraisals were often cursory. Insurers were lulled into complacency as they saw comfortable profits pile up year after year on the homeowners policies they sold.

But things were quietest before the storms—

the literal storms of the 1990s. A virtual plague of catastrophes has rained down on U.S. homeowners since then and has changed the face of these policies for the foreseeable future.

Oakland, California, suffered devastating fires in 1991. In August 1992 Hurricane Andrew ripped through Florida, Louisiana, and Mississippi and earned its stripes as the costliest disaster in U.S. history, inflicting losses of $15.5 billion. A month later Hurricane Iniki ravaged Hawaii. During the summer of 1993, the Midwest suffered debilitating floods. Early one morning in January 1994, residents of Southern California were awakened by the Northridge earthquake, which caused some $12.5 billion in damage. And the winter of 1996 saw snowfall records toppled throughout the Northeast: damage estimates were running at $1.995 billion at last count, according to the American Insurance Services Group. In all, 7 of the 10 costliest catastrophes in U.S. history have occurred since 1990.

Why does this affect your rates if you never filed a claim? When insurers pay out record claims, real concerns arise about their solvency. In Florida seven insurers went bankrupt in Andrew's aftermath. And many consumers found they were not properly insured: for instance, only about 20 percent of the Midwest flood victims had any flood insurance at all.

In the past year or two, homeowners insurance has become almost impossible to get in some areas. California consumers have found themselves in the middle of a genuine crisis, as companies serving some 93 percent of the market effectively withdrew from writing new policies. Many policyholders found non-renewal notices in their mailboxes, forcing them to shop for new insurers. Those unable to find companies willing to take them had to turn to the state insurance pool, the insurer of last resort. But those policies, says Richard Wiebe, a spokesman for the California Dept. of Insurance, offer only "bare-bones coverage at high prices."

Consumers who could keep their insurance saw premiums go up, about 30 percent in California on average. Premiums for earthquake policies alone went up 100 to 150 percent. Florida residents saw similar results after Hurricane Andrew. There, the statewide average for premiums is up 63 percent since 1993, while some homeowners in the hardest-hit counties, such as Dade and Broward, have seen premiums double or triple. As companies refused to write new insurance, the state of Florida set up an insurance pool, which quickly ballooned to become the third-largest insurer in the state.

The impact has been felt beyond those two states: residents along the eastern seaboard have found insurers reluctant to write policies. Across the country, membership has jumped in the state-run insurance pools that are sponsored by 31 states and the District of Columbia. Insurance companies are revamping application procedures, increasing mandatory deductibles, and increasingly rejecting applicants they deem risky. "May you live in interesting times," says the ancient Chinese curse.

☞ **As long as we are on the subject, you're probably not covered for floods and earthquakes.**
Homeowners insurance covers you for calamities such as fire, windstorm, hail, a vehicle running into your house, robbery or vandalism, or damage from falling objects or from the weight of snow and ice. But it's important to note what is specifically excluded—most significantly, floods and earthquakes. If you live in a region where your home is at risk for either, you will need to add on a special policy to cover those areas.

Flood insurance is available through the National Flood Insurance Program (800-638-6620). The government estimates that two-thirds of the buildings that should carry flood insurance don't. To qualify you must live in one of the 20,000 communities that have agreed to abide by Federal Emergency Management Agency (FEMA) guidelines, which are designed to reduce flood losses. Homes are covered for replacement cost up to $250,000 (if your house is destroyed, to collect what it would cost to replace it, you must have insured it for at least 80 percent of that estimated cost and you must live in the home at least 80 percent of the time), but your personal possessions can be covered only for actual cash value, up to a maximum of $100,000. Although flood insurance is administered by a federal program, 95 percent of the policies are sold by insurance agents and companies, while only 5 percent are purchased directly through the National Flood Insurance Program.

Although it may seem like an obvious point, be aware that insurers aren't interested in taking applications for flood insurance at the last minute. The time to call is not when water is rising in the basement and the police are evacuating your town. There is a 30-day waiting period before flood insurance takes effect, except in specific circumstances. One such case is when you're a new homeowner and your mortgage company requires flood insurance.

If you live in California, earthquake insurance is a necessity. The state currently requires companies that sell homeowners insurance to make earthquake insurance available as well. That requirement has prompted many insurers to stop writing new policies in California altogether. There are also anecdotal reports of companies informally (and illegally) agreeing to sell homeowners coverage only if the customer promises not to request earthquake coverage. Homeowners who are unable to get insurance must turn to the state's FAIR (Fair Access to Insurance Requirements) program, which is an insurer of last resort. (See the "State-by-State Guide," page 218.)

For those who do manage to procure earthquake insurance, a typical California deductible is 10 percent of the damage (in Missouri, where the New Madrid fault also raises earthquake risks, the deductible is typically 5 percent), and certain types of buildings, such as older ones or those made of brick, are more expensive to insure than, say, new wood-frame buildings.

☞ **The single most important phrase you can learn is this: guaranteed replacement-cost coverage.**
Chant it to your agent or insurer when you're signing up for a policy. Replacement cost means that if catastrophe strikes, the insurer will pay to replace your house and contents and not just give you a check for the face value of the policy. Why is that so important? The cost to rebuild and

replace your home may be higher than the face value.

One common misconception about homeowners insurance is that a house should be insured for its market value, or perhaps for what you paid for it. For insurance purposes, the market value of your dwelling is irrelevant, since it includes the cost of the land, which doesn't need insuring: even if a fire incinerated your house, you'd still own the land underneath all the rubble and ashes.

And market values are notoriously volatile: your home may be worth less than it was a few years ago and less than it would cost to replace. Whatever the current state of your local real-estate market, the cost of rebuilding a house rarely goes down. If your home burns or is tossed around the county by a tornado, you need the money to rebuild, not just the amount you could sell it for.

Some insurance companies build guaranteed replacement-cost value into a policy, perhaps as part of a package of endorsements (enhancements to your basic policy that give you additional coverage for your property). Others charge an additional 10 percent or so to add it on.

The main point is this: don't automatically assume that you have this coverage. In general, if you haven't requested it, or an agent hasn't suggested it, you don't have it. Make certain you ask for guaranteed replacement, and when your policy arrives in the mail, check to see it's included.

Why so emphatic about this? Because although your insurance company will try to judge what it would cost to rebuild your house and insure it for that amount, that figure can fluctuate. If there's a widespread loss, like a hurricane or fire that inflicts damage on many homes, materials and labor become scarce and costs can skyrocket.

☞ Get inside your policy, and use these general guides for coverage.
The best way to provide shelter for yourself and your investment is to familiarize yourself with the basics. Your homeowners policy covers your:

1. house

2. personal property. For lack of a better phrase, this means all your stuff—your furniture, your clothing, your stereo system, your grandmother's silver

3. other structures on your property—your shed, a mailbox, a satellite dish, a garage, and other structures detached from your home. The limit for coverage on these is usually about 10 percent of the coverage on your house. So if your home is insured for $100,000, the most the outbuildings will be covered for is $10,000

4. landscaping—the plants, trees, and shrubs on your property. These are typically covered for up to 5 percent of the insurance value of the house, to a maximum of $500 per item. But note that coverage isn't for damage done by wind, only the other hazards named in your policy

5. loss of use. If you can't live in your house, your policy will pay temporary living expenses until you can move back in. The typical limit on this provision is up to 20 percent of the insured value of your home

6. liability. This is "slip and fall" coverage, useful if guests or passersby fall on your front steps and injure themselves. It also travels with you; if you're riding your bike and do some damage, your homeowners liability will cover you. Typical levels are $100,000 or $300,000, but most consumers should consider getting additional coverage in the form of umbrella liability (see page 59).

☞ **Homeowners policies are standardized—but you still must keep an eye out for subtle differences.**

Homeowners insurance is typically sold in six or seven basic varieties, which differ in the kind and amount of coverage they offer. HO-3 (which stands for "homeowners 3"), for example, is the most popular homeowners policy, while HO-4 is the policy aimed at renters, and HO-6 is for condominium owners.

These standardized policy forms are drawn up by the consulting firms that provide research, statistical, and actuarial information to insurance companies. The most dominant of these firms are the New York–based Insurance Services

Office (ISO) and the American Association of Insurance Services (AAIS). Another group, the MSO, or Mutual Services Office, provides forms for many smaller mutual insurers.

These forms provide standard templates for homeowners coverage that can be used to compare one company's policy with another's. However, some firms add their own bells and whistles. "Even the big insurers, which use their own forms, stick pretty closely to the standard ones," says David Fairweather, a vice president for underwriting for Amica, a direct writer of homeowners insurance. "But we do see some product differentiation on small things. Some companies may offer a higher limit on how much jewelry they'll cover." So though policy numbers will give you a general idea of what's covered, for the specifics you need to review the policy itself.

For a quick overview of what perils the typical policies cover, you can study the chart on the following page. A few quick notes: HO-1, the basic, bare-bones homeowners policy, is rarely sold these days. Other policies offering broader coverage are standard.

Most states follow this format, with the notable exception of Texas. There, three homeowners-insurance forms are available, with terms mandated by the state. They are:

1. HO-A, which covers your home and its contents against the named perils only, for their actual cash value

2. HO-B, which covers your house and its contents against the named perils. Unlike HO-A, HO-B covers your house for replacement-cost value and the contents for actual cash value, unless you buy additional replacement coverage

3. HO-C, the most generous—and expensive—of the policies, provides the same extent of coverage for your house and its contents as HO-B. The difference is that you are covered for all risks that aren't specifically excluded.

☞ **Get replacement-cost-value insurance for the contents of your home, too.**
Typically, insurers estimate that the personal belongings of families are worth about 70 percent of the face value of the

HOMEOWNERS' PERILS

PERILS

Fire or lightning

Windstorm or hail

Explosion

Riot or civil commotion

Aircraft

Vehicles

Smoke

Vandalism or malicious mischief

Theft

Damage done by glass or safety glazing material that is part of a building

Volcanic eruption

Falling objects

Weight of ice, snow, or sleet

Accidental discharge or overflow of water from within a plumbing,
    heating, air-conditioning, or automatic fire-protective
    sprinkler system, or from within a household appliance

Sudden and accidental tearing apart, cracking, burning, or bulging
    of a steam or hot-water heating system, air-conditioning,
    or automatic fire-protective sprinkler system

Freezing of a plumbing, heating, air-conditioning, or automatic
    fire-protective sprinkler system, or of a household appliance

Sudden and accidental damage from artificially generated
    electrical current (does not include loss of a tube, transistor,
    or similar electronic component)

All perils except flood, earthquake, war, nuclear accident, and
    others specified in your policy. Check your policy for a complete
    listing of perils excluded

● dwelling & personal property   ■ dwelling only   ▲ personal property only

BASIC HO-1	BROAD HO-2	SPECIAL HO-3	RENTER'S HO-4	UNIT OWNER'S HO-6	OLDER HOME HO-8
●	●	●	▲	▲	●
●	●	●	▲	▲	●
●	●	●	▲	▲	●
●	●	●	▲	▲	●
●	●	●	▲	▲	●
●	●	●	▲	▲	●
●	●	●	▲	▲	●
●	●	●	▲	▲	●
●	●	●	▲	▲	●
●	●	●	▲	▲	●
	●	●	▲	▲	
	●	●	▲	▲	
	●	●	▲	▲	
	●	●	▲	▲	
	●	●	▲	▲	
	●	●	▲	▲	
		■			

SOURCE: INSURANCE INFORMATION INSTITUTE

insurance policy and write personal-property insurance for that amount. But replacement-cost-value coverage is important for your household goods, as well.

Actual cash value is depreciated value. A refrigerator that originally cost $1,000 might be worth only $300 after 10 or 11 years. If you lost that fridge in a fire and had actual-cash-value insurance on your belongings, you'd get only a few hundred dollars for it. What about your five-year-old television and your four-year-old sofa? You can bet that the check you'd get for their current depreciated value would be a lot less than the check you'd have to write to replace them.

☞ **Be aware that guaranteed replacement cost increasingly means different things to different companies.** "Some companies say we'll pay to rebuild it, period," says Douglas Kroh, a former insurance agent who now teaches the subject to agents and college students. "But others have instituted caps on how much they'll pay. They might range from 125 percent of the face value of the policy to 200 percent of the face value." That's a huge difference: That means on a $100,000 house, your coverage would range from $125,000 to $200,000—or higher, if there's no cap. Review your policy to make sure you know what your limits are.

☞ **Marshall & Swift, a Los Angeles consulting firm that estimates construction costs nationally for insurers, thinks that a full 70 percent of the homes in this country are underinsured—by an average of 30 to 31 percent—mostly because of underappraisals. Make sure your home isn't one of them.**
When you buy homeowners coverage, the agent or company will place a value on what it would cost to rebuild your home in the event of a total loss. Even though you've made sure you have guaranteed replacement-cost insurance (with, it is hoped, no caps), it's still important to put an accurate value on the house.

As mentioned earlier, it doesn't matter how much you

paid for your house or what its market value is. Merely looking at local per-square-foot building costs can be misleading, too. These don't include costs for demolition or debris removal (which typically add perhaps 10 percent to the cost of building a home), and they may well be for the cheapest available construction, while your home may be of higher quality.

Your insurance company or agent may do an in-person appraisal or may ask you a series of questions to determine what the face value of your homeowners should be. You can also get an independent real-estate appraiser to give you an estimate of what it would cost to rebuild, a step that might make sense if you have a more expensive, one-of-a-kind, or custom-built home. Among the factors that enter into a home's insurance cost are its age (generally, the older the house, the more expensive to rebuild), its size, its construction quality, and its style.

Marshall & Swift's estimates are based on several factors, including comparisons of what insurance companies have actually paid out to rebuild with what the homes were insured for. Some of the widespread underinsurance the firm finds is the result of simple miscalculations (reporting the size of the home incorrectly, for example) or incorrect descriptions of a home's style or construction quality. But with insurers capping guaranteed replacement values, getting the right figure is more important than ever.

Once you have an idea of how much your home would cost to rebuild, make sure you insure it for 100 percent of that amount. Insurers will allow you to buy less than full coverage, but if you do, they won't pay full replacement value, even on partial losses. Say you have a small fire and it does damage that would cost $10,000 to repair; if you're insured for only 50 percent of the $100,000 value of your home, the insurer may pay only the actual cash value of the items damaged, rather than their $10,000 replacement cost.

☞ **One big note of caution: Don't make the mistake of buying only enough coverage to pay off the mortgage.**
Mortgage lenders usually require homeowners insurance, but only enough to ensure they get their money back. That's generally not enough for your purposes. Again, the relevant phrase is guaranteed cost replacement.

☞ **Find out if your insurance will pay to rebuild your house to meet local zoning laws and ordinances.**
This is an arcane-sounding consideration, but ignoring it could cost you a bundle. Communities have minimum building standards. These could be updated to require, for instance, certain types of wiring or construction that an existing home wouldn't have. If you had to rebuild, you'd be forced to comply with those new standards, but your homeowners policy might pay only to replace what you had, not what you're now required to have.

Such requirements vary and can be expensive. An older home may need an updated electrical system, while a homeowner in another community might be required to install a fire sprinkler system or to reinforce the roof to resist hurricanes, and in coastal areas a house may need to be moved to a higher elevation.

If your policy doesn't cover zoning and ordinance updates, you may need an endorsement or rider to provide the coverage. This is especially important for an older home. Florida now requires insurers to provide an additional 25 percent of a home's face-value coverage to pay for ordinance claims, and many companies provide 10 percent of face-value coverage for zoning and ordinance coverage in their standard endorsements, but both dollar limits may be low if your house needs major upgrading.

☞ **Review your coverage regularly.**
Once you've determined the replacement cost of your home, you can't file away your policy and forget it. If you improve your house, or add on to it, you'll need to increase your insurance. A rule of thumb is that if you've put more than $5,000

into it, or increased its value by 5 percent, you probably need
more coverage. Some companies require this.

And building costs go up every year. Check that the policy has some sort of inflation rider or endorsement so that
as costs rise, your coverage automatically follows them.

It's important not to let an inflation-guard endorsement
overinsure your home. Some companies use a 6 to 8 percent
inflation guard though local costs might go up only 2 to 4
percent. "I recommend doing a new cost estimate every
three or four years," says Kroh. "Too much insurance means
too high a premium."

☞ Know your policy's limits.

Your homeowners policy limits coverage on certain items.
Policies differ somewhat, but the amounts listed below are
typically the maximum an insurer will reimburse you if
these items are lost, stolen, or destroyed:

◆ $200 for money, bank notes, gold and silver, coins, and
   medals
◆ $1,000 on securities, accounts, deeds, passports, tickets,
   stamps
◆ $1,000 on watercraft, including trailers and equipment
◆ $1,000 on trailers not used for watercraft
◆ $1,000 for jewelry, watches, furs, and precious and semi-
   precious stones
◆ $2,500 for silverware, silverplate, goldware, pewterware
◆ $2,500 on property used for business at home and $250
   on property damaged or lost while traveling
◆ $2,500 on firearms

If your silverware drawer, jewelry box, or attic contains
treasures that are worth more than these limits, ask your
insurer about buying a rider. Some policies also have strict
limits on reimbursement for artwork, antiques, oriental
rugs, musical instruments, and camera or sporting equipment. Riders will provide insurance for the things you specify. One big plus: riders are "all-risk" insurance. Your jewelry is covered even if you simply lose it, while under a

general homeowners policy, there has to be a good chance of theft in order to recover.

To buy a rider, you'll need a professional, written appraisal of an item or a bill of sale describing it. "If someone reports a stolen diamond ring, it doesn't do us much good," says Amica's Fairweather. "But a bill of sale will tell us things like how many carats the diamond was and will describe the setting, the cut, and the clarity." If you don't have a receipt, jewelry stores will usually provide a written description and appraisal of an item for insurance purposes. Appraisers for other items can be located through the American Society of Appraisers (703-478-2228) or the Appraisers Association of America (212-889-5404).

👉 **Few homeowners policies cover animal damage or other weird things.**

A prime example is damage done by your pet. Douglas Kroh relates a claim he once handled: "The family had a large dog, which climbed the pull-down ladder into the attic and proceeded to try to bury a bone in the insulation in the attic, digging away. The dog dug through the living-room ceiling and dropped through to the floor." Neither the dog nor the surprised family were hurt. On the other hand, the living-room ceiling and attic insulation were demolished. But the family wasn't eligible to file a claim.

Damage done by other animals may also fall outside your policy. If a rodent chews through your electrical wiring or termites burrow into your wood framing, you're probably on your own.

And if your sewers or drains back up, it's not normally covered, unless an endorsement addresses the possibility. That means if a tree root grows into the pipes in your yard, or your unruly toddler flushes a towel down the toilet and you have water or sewage backed up in your carpeted, paneled basement, the insurer won't pay your claim.

LIABILITY COVERAGE

GETTING SUED IS A FACT OF modern life. The dispute could be over a neighbor slipping on your front steps, a golf ball gone astray, or your dog biting someone. If you were sued and found liable for damage or injury caused to someone, the liability portion of your homeowners policy would pay for your legal defense and for any damages assessed against you, up to the policy limit. If you don't have liability insurance, that judgment and the lawyers' fees would come out of your assets.

To be covered, damage must be unintentional or accidental. Insurers aren't going to fund a blood feud between you and your neighbor. Insurers also won't pay for your legal costs in a criminal matter.

In the past, policies provided for $100,000 in liability, but that's increasingly being upgraded to $300,000. The cost to increase coverage from $100,000 to $300,000 is typically about $15 a year, small change for the additional security it provides. Most homeowners should insist on a minimum of $300,000 in coverage, and for many, additional umbrella liability coverage makes sense. This covers you after you have exhausted the liability included under your homeowners and auto policies. Most umbrella policies provide $1 million of coverage for a reasonable $150 to $300 a year. And they cover situations that regular liability insurance doesn't. An umbrella policy can protect you if you are sued for insulting someone in a nasty letter to the editor, for instance.

Umbrella liability can also provide coverage for other legal problems. President Clinton's umbrella liability insurers, State Farm and Chubb, have paid out about $900,000 so far toward his legal costs in the sexual-harassment suit brought against him by Paula Jones. Increasingly, though, insurers are specifically excluding coverage for sexual-harassment suits.

Umbrella liability insurance usually excludes your

business and professional activities. If you're a physician, it is not a substitute for malpractice insurance, for instance.

☞ **One note about that aggressive dog.**
Insurance companies will usually pay for one dog bite. Repeated incidents are likely to motivate your insurer not to renew your coverage.

☞ **More than 60 percent of renters have no coverage. If you are a renter, get it today.**
As older and more affluent consumers rent, the importance of renters insurance grows. However, though the number of people who have renters insurance has gone up in the past few years, the percentages are still appallingly low. If you're a renter, you need to protect your personal belongings. If there's a fire, for instance, your landlord probably has insurance to cover the damage to the building, but it won't cover your ruined furniture.

But the real reason you need some kind of insurance is for the liability coverage. Without coverage all your assets are at risk if you're sued. Even if you're young and don't have significant assets yet, you may not be safe: there have been judgments that include a person's future earnings. Don't overlook the fact that if you cause or contribute to damage to your apartment building (say, you fall asleep while something is cooking in the oven and a fire starts), your landlord probably can sue you under the terms of your lease.

A renters policy (the HO-4 version of homeowners) is fairly cheap, about $150 a year for $25,000 to $40,000 of contents coverage and $300,000 of liability coverage. The policyholder has the same choice as homeowners do between replacement-cost and cash-value coverage. Pay the extra for replacement-cost coverage. If you own expensive jewelry or computer equipment, ask specifically about coverage limits and consider purchasing a rider.

Likewise, renters have to decide how much of a deductible they're willing to pay before collecting on a claim. As usual, the higher the deductible, the lower the premium.

☞ You need different insurance on a condominium than on a house.

Your condominium agreement will help you determine what insurance you need. Condo dwellers own what's inside their walls, so all owners need the standard personal-property coverage for furniture and belongings and the standard liability coverage. But different agreements require different levels of insurance beyond this. Under some, you may need to insure everything from the unpainted Sheetrock of the exterior walls in. So, for example, built-in bookcases would be on your coverage. Other documents are written so that owners must insure "all nonbearing walls and bearing walls, from studs out." That means that in the event of a fire, you'd have to replace your own Sheetrock.

Your condominium association will purchase insurance on the actual buildings and property, as well as liability coverage for the general association. Beyond this, there are gray areas. Some condos require you to cover your own appliances, cabinets, and so forth. Others include such items in their coverage and state as much in their bylaws.

The best way to make sure your condo coverage meshes properly with your condominium development's agreement is to give a copy of the agreement to your insurance agent or company. That way the insurer can determine proper coverage.

Condo owners, as well as anyone in some type of home-owners-association complex, can also buy loss-assessment insurance, which will cover any excess assessments that the association hits you with. If the condominium clubhouse burned and the association was underinsured, you'd be assessed a fee. Loss-assessment coverage would pay that fee. However, it won't pay for routine maintenance or upgrades, only for damages that would normally be covered under the insurance policy.

☞ Increase your homeowners deductibles, and watch those claims.

Not only will a higher deductible cut your insurance premium (raising your deductible from $100 to $1,000 could earn you a discount of 35 percent), but it will discourage you from making small claims. That's important because submitting too many claims—however well documented or justified—can make your insurer not want you anymore. It can decide not to renew your policy, or it can raise your rates. Individual weather-related claims don't cause insurers to drop policyholders, but too many theft or fire claims might.

"Don't use your homeowners for maintenance," suggests Douglas Kroh. "If you have a $250 deductible and a $275 loss, don't put in a claim for $25." If you want to put in a claim and you're unsure about what the impact will be on your insurance, ask.

"In my area of Texas, two nonweather claims will cause a surcharge on your insurance, with three causing a nonrenewal," says Houston agent Larry Lipton.

☞ There's no getting around it: you must take the time to must do a home inventory.

If you have a catastrophe, a Rolls-Royce of a homeowners policy won't be much use if you can't place an accurate and detailed claim.

Most of us can't remember where we put our car keys, much less reconstruct, from memory, the entire contents of closets, attic, and cabinets. The best record is an inventory of your belongings, along with serial numbers, purchase prices, and dates of purchase.

Until you find time to do that, there are some other easy steps you can take. For one thing, save receipts from major purchases, so you have a price and an item description.

Go around your home, room by room, with a camera or video camera, and record everything. Open kitchen cabinets, closets, and drawers, and photograph the contents. Don't overlook draperies, rugs, lamps, or the artwork on your walls. Do the basement, attic, and garage. You own more than you think you do. In an emergency, a film record will jog your memory and provide real evidence.

Once you have an inventory, store a copy somewhere off your premises—in a bank safety-deposit box or at a friend's or family member's house. If you have a fire, you don't want your inventory to go up in smoke.

☞ **Equipment used at home for business purposes is usually covered only up to an unrealistically low level, such as $2,500.**

A home office with a computer, printer, fax machine, and copier can easily cost more than $2,500 to replace. So look into special home-office coverage. There are liability reasons to get this, too. If a client is hurt while visiting your home office, your homeowners liability may not cover the accident. Ask your insurer about home-office insurance. Coverage is available either as a rider to your existing policy or in a separate policy. Talk to your insurer about which is appropriate for your business. A consultant who works out of a spare bedroom and doesn't meet clients at home may only need a rider to his or her homeowners policy. A home-based business that manufactures and sells a product may need the additional liability coverage that a stand-alone policy provides. One company offers a separate at-home business policy that provides $300,000 in liability, $10,000 in contents (equipment), and 12 months' worth of "reasonable" business-interruption coverage, which would typically be used to cover the cost of renting an office outside the home until your home office was usable again. The annual premium for the policy: $150 a year.

☞ **When you insure your vacation cottage, remember that your personal-liability coverage may be provided by the insurance on your primary home, so you probably only need insurance on the property.**

That can save you money on your premium. Check with your insurer to see if it will extend your liability. But if you rent out your vacation home, you may need extra liability on your primary policy. Keep in mind that the more remote your property is, and the further it is from a fire department, the higher the premium will be. Homeowner-policy premiums are the reverse of those for auto: rural rates may be higher than suburban or urban rates, because of the inaccessibility to a fire department.

👉 Use your discounts to save money.

◆ Smoke detectors and security systems in your house can help you qualify for discounts—up to 20 percent for sophisticated fire/burglar alarm systems.

◆ A new home may entitle you to discounts, assuming that it is in good condition (the roof isn't worn and ripe for leaking) and meets current building codes. Amica, for instance, gives a 20 percent discount on homes that are one to two years old. That discount drops by 2 percent each year, disappearing entirely after year 10.

◆ Consolidate your insurance business. Insuring your car and your home with the same company can get you a discount.

◆ If you've updated or renovated your home with modern materials, which tend to be more fire-resistant than older ones, notify your insurer. You might qualify for some discounts.

◆ Don't smoke. A few companies offer discounts if there are no smokers in the household.

◆ Ask if your company offers a discount to longtime policy-holders. Some will cut your premium by 5 percent if you've insured through them for three to five years, and by 10 percent if you've been a customer for six years or more.

👉 You can can get service and coverage that is every bit as good by going through a direct-quote insurer, rather than an agent.

Many people prefer to deal with a local agent they know, but consumer-satisfaction surveys show a preference for direct-quote insurers, such as USAA (800-531-8100) and

Amica (800-242-6422). In shopping around for coverage, try getting quotes from them as well as from State Farm and Allstate, which have the largest share of the U.S. homeowners insurance market. If you deal with an independent agent, you should expect him or her to get quotes from several companies for you, not just one.

☞ **Your credit record does have an impact on your homeowners insurance.**

Some companies will look at your credit record to judge whether to sell you homeowners insurance, and it is legal to deny you coverage on the basis of your record. Insurers reason that policyholders with financial problems have an incentive to file inflated or fraudulent claims.

If you think you are being discriminated against, call your state insurance department. Sometimes it can bring pressure on the company or help direct you to another firm. Some states are enacting laws to prohibit this use of credit reports.

☞ **Don't lie on your application. CLUE is watching you.**

When you apply for homeowners insurance, the company or agent will ask if you've had any claims during the past three years. As few as two or three noncatastrophe claims

10 LARGEST HOME INSURERS

COMPANY	% OF MARKET SHARE
State Farm Group	23.6%
Allstate Insurance Group	11.9%
Farmers Insurance Group	5.7%
USAA Group	3.2%
Nationwide Group	2.95%
Chubb Group of Insurance Cos.	2.0%
Aetna Life & Casualty Group	1.9%
Prudential of America Group	1.9%
Safeco Insurance Cos.	1.7%
ITT/Hartford Insurance Group	1.6%

SOURCE: A.M. BEST

are enough to convince many insurers not to cover you. (If
you were in the path of a tornado, it would not raise eye-
brows in the same way that three house fires might.)

But don't be tempted to conveniently forget past claims.
Equifax, the credit-reporting firm, has a service called CLUE
(Comprehensive Loss Underwriting Exchange), which oper-
ates a little like the medical-insurance bureaus. Insurers
report what claims have been paid at what addresses, and
agents and companies can do a database search on new
applicants.

If you're denied coverage because of CLUE, you're entitled
to a free copy of your report. Like credit reports and medical
information bureau reports, CLUE reports can contain inaccurate information about you.

☞ **If you can't get homeowners insurance, try your
state insurance department.**
Thirty-one states and the District of Columbia have FAIR
plans for homeowners who are unable to get insurance
through the private markets. The numbers of all the state
insurance agencies are listed in the "State-by-State Guide,"
page 218.

☞ **But you can legally be denied insurance, even
through one of these plans.**
For obvious reasons, anyone convicted in the past five years
of arson or of the use of explosives or destruction of property can be denied coverage. If your property taxes are more
than two years overdue, if your property is being used for
illegal purposes, or if you've had a policy canceled for non-
payment in the past two years, forget it. A house that has
been vacant for an extended period of time can also be difficult to insure.

☞ **If you are a victim of a catastrophe, expect to
encounter a public adjuster.**
This is a person who will help you file a claim with your
insurance company and negotiate with it in exchange for a

cut—usually about 15 percent of the claim, though you can probably get below that. Adjusters claim that they can boost your reimbursement by enough to pay for their fee.

There are good public adjusters, and there are some infamous scamsters in this business, too. If you hire one, make sure he or she is licensed by the state insurance department and has time to devote to your claim. Ironically, the worst time to hire one of these people is when there has been a widespread disaster, like a hurricane.

"In Florida we saw public adjusters come in and sign up as many people as they could, and all they were doing was taking what the insurance company offered and taking their percentage off the top," says Ina DeLong, the president of United Policyholders, a San Francisco–based consumers group. "There are situations where I think a public adjuster would be an excellent choice, but you have to prequalify them and ask for references."

Remember, you're always free to hire a public adjuster after you've had an initial offer from your insurer. At that point, you can negotiate to pay the adjuster based on what he or she gets you in excess of the insurance company's initial offer.

CHAPTER

Health
INSURANCE

Pepping Up Your Policy

AN EXECUTIVE who had open heart surgery last year is currently covered by his company's group health insurance, but he worries. His firm is going to be laying off workers. How could he get affordable health insurance with a preexisting heart condition?

A New Jersey mother rushes her daughter to the hospital emergency room when the teenager cuts her hand badly opening a can of cat food while caring for a neighbor's pet. A doctor there stitches not only the skin but the underlying tissue. The insurer balks at paying for two rows of stitches: its treatment codes indicate that only one was called for. Despite weeks of calls and letters, the insurer stands firm, and the neighbor offers to pay the difference. "I'm convinced that one way they control health-care costs is to make it so difficult to get reimbursement that the

employee gives up and pays out of his own pocket," the mother says.

A woman suffering from breast cancer is advised that her best chance at remission would come from having a bone-marrow transplant. But bone-marrow transplants, though common and approved for other cancerous conditions, such as leukemia, are still considered experimental for breast cancer. The insurer won't pay.

An accountant and his chronically ill wife relocate to another state, where he has a job offer.

Under the new company's health-insurance policy, her illness is considered a "preexisting condition" and is not eligible for coverage for a year.

An emergency-room worker frets. He's the one who places calls to managed-care companies to obtain approval for incoming patients. Of the dozen or so HMOs he deals with, one or two, he's convinced, deliberately understaff their telephone lines. "We call dozens of times, and the line is always busy. Meanwhile patients are waiting for care or getting care that they don't know if they're covered for."

WELCOME TO HEALTH INSURANCE in the 1990s—frustrating, annoying, and scary. No wonder most of us would prefer not to think about it. But that's a luxury we can't afford. Today, more than ever, having good health insurance is vital. It is the safety net that everyone needs. Without it even a short hospitalization could send you into a financial free-fall. It also ensures access to care: although hospitals are legally required to provide emergency treatment to all who require it, it is naive to think that an uninsured patient gets the same quality of care, either routine or emergency, that an insured patient gets.

How do you get good coverage? The uncertainties of the job market, employers' unwillingness to foot increasingly expensive insurance bills, and the multiplication of policy types and variations make the task far from easy. Rule No. 1, though, is to get and stay insured. Don't assume that because you've never had a serious illness, you or someone in your family won't have one, or that because you're over 65 and covered by Medicare, Uncle Sam will take care of all your bills. And don't let your coverage lapse when you're laid off or switching jobs.

Rule No. 2 is to make sure you understand what each type of policy entails in the way of costs, coverage, and restrictions. Then you have to ask yourself which variety best suits your resources and needs. That will depend on whether you get group insurance through your employer or have to insure yourself, what your income is, and whether you're eligible for some sort of government assistance.

HOW WE GOT HERE

IF THERE WERE EVER A REASON to be nostalgic for the good old days, health insurance is it. Once—not much more than a decade or so ago—your employer picked up the tab for your health-insurance costs. In return you paid a small deductible (the amount of covered expenses you are responsible for each year before your insurer will pay claims), of $100 or so, and had your choice of doctors and hospitals. If your condition required you to see a specialist, you chose one, went, and sent the bill to the insurance company, which paid it.

Those days, of course, have gone the way of penny candy and buggy whips. Such generosity got killed by skyrocketing medical bills. The cost of providing health care has risen faster than the rate of inflation for most of the past 25 years, pushed up in part by malpractice suits that forced doctors to practice defensive, and expensive, medicine. Technology also played a role, as doctors and hospitals justified their purchase of expensive new equipment by ordering often-unnecessary tests. Meanwhile, patients came to expect cutting-edge treatment, no matter what their prognosis.

Insurance companies, inefficient and angling for profits, simply passed on their costs to corporate and individual consumers. Soon, though, they'd hiked premiums to the point where employers couldn't, or wouldn't, pay them. As a result, the percentage of businesses not offering health insurance has risen. An estimated 72 percent of employers with fewer than 25 employees offered no health insurance in

1993, the latest year for which statistics are available. That's up from 69 percent just four years earlier. And if you're one of the individuals forced to buy your own coverage, heaven help you. It's expensive and hard to get if you have a history of illness. The upshot: at last count, in 1994, 39 million Americans were uninsured, according to the Employee Benefits Research Institute.

Those who are still insured have had to shoulder a bigger share of their health-care costs and accept more limited coverage. Employee contributions (the amount employees must chip in from their paychecks for coverage), deductibles, and copayments (the amount or percentage of bills they're required to pay) have all risen. And managed care, the catchall phrase for the various types of cost-saving strategies that insurers and employers are trying to implement, has become the order of the day. According to a 1995 study by employee-benefits consultant Foster Higgins, the portion of employees enrolled in some form of managed-care plan rose from 63 percent in 1994 to 71 percent in 1995.

"Basically everyone in a health-insurance plan today is subject to some elements of managed care," says Charles Inlander, president of the People's Medical Society, a consumer health-care group. "It may range from having to get surgical procedures and hospital admissions preapproved to being in an HMO where all treatment and referrals must come from your primary physician. But everybody is in some managed-care plan."

The good news is that cost-saving measures, mostly implemented through managed-care plans, seem to be working: in 1995, for the first time in 10 years, growth in private-sector medical-care premiums fell below the rate of overall inflation. The bad news is that consumers have had to cope with other consequences, ranging from the inconvenience of hassling with insurers to life-threatening examples of care being withheld.

WHAT'S YOUR PLAN?

THOUGH INSURERS HAVE DEVISED all sorts of hybrids of different types of health plans, there are four basic models for health-insurance coverage in the United States today: the indemnity plan, the health maintenance organization, the preferred provider organization, and the point-of-service plan.

The indemnity plan: This is the traditional fee-for-service model, much beloved by patients and doctors but despised by insurers and by employers, who foot most of the bill. Indemnity plans were the most common form of employer-provided health insurance until the early 1990s, when managed-care plans began to grow. Today, in return for the flexibility of choosing your own caregivers and consulting specialists without prior approval from the insurance company, you may pay higher employee contributions, copayments, and deductibles than you would in other types of plans. A survey by Foster Higgins found that 61 percent of companies have deductibles of $500 or more. In most cases, you also pay 20 percent coinsurance, or copayments for medical (doctor's fees) and hospital services.

Indemnity plans, though, have out-of-pocket maximums limiting how much you have to pay in any one year: once your deductible and copayments exceed a certain level, the insurance company begins to pick up 100 percent of the cost, rather than 80 percent. In 1995 the average out-of-pocket maximum for a family was $2,600. However, the insurer also imposes lifetime maximum limits on its payouts, after which it won't cover any more care.

The health maintenance organization: HMOs range from stand-alone clinics, staffed by groups of physicians who take care of all the health needs of their patients, to looser confederations of doctors located in different offices. They are usually cheaper than other types of health plans, both when provided by an employer and when coverage is purchased individually. You pay no deductibles, file no insurance claims forms, and are subject to only modest copayments ($9 on average per doctor visit in 1995); there is no lifetime payout maximum. In return, however, you are restricted to the HMO's physicians, hospitals, and specialists.

PLANS AT A GLANCE

Indemnity plans:
◆ Offer freedom of choice among physicians
◆ Usually require contributions from employees
◆ In most cases require 20 percent copayment for medical and hospital services
◆ Have ever-increasing deductibles; $500, on average, for family, $200 for an individual
◆ Have out-of-pocket maximums; $2,600, on average, for a family, $1,300 for individuals
◆ Have lifetime maximum payouts
◆ In 1995 cost, on average, $3,650 per year

Health Maintenance Organizations (HMOs):
◆ Only cover care given by doctors in the network; treatment by outside physicians not reimbursed
◆ May require employee contributions
◆ In most cases have no deductible
◆ Require a small copayment; $9, on average, for office visits
◆ Typically do not have lifetime maximum payouts or out-of-pocket maximums
◆ In 1995 cost, on average, $3,255

The preferred provider organization: PPOs consist of networks of doctors and hospitals. If you belong to one, you can choose a provider within its network, or you can go outside for care. In either case, you are liable for copayments and deductibles, but the charges are lower if you use an approved provider. According to Foster Higgins, the average individual deductible is $200 for in-network care, $250 for out-of-network services; families' deductibles are $500. In-network coinsurance payments are usually 10 to 20 percent of expenses, although plans sometimes

Preferred Provider Organizations (PPOs):
◆ Have incentives to use network doctors and facilities but provide some coverage for out-of-network care
◆ May require employee contributions
◆ Have deductibles; about $200 individual and $500 family for in-network care, $250 and $500 for out-of-network care
◆ Require copayments; $10 per visit in-network, or 10 to 20 percent of charges, and an average of 30 percent out-of-network
◆ Have out-of-pocket maximums; $1,200 in-network and $2,000 out-of-network, on average, for individuals, $2,100 and $3,450 for families
◆ In 1995 cost, on average, $3,169

Point-Of-Services (POSs):
◆ Have a deductible for out-of-network care ($300 individual, $600 family); none in-network
◆ May require employee contributions
◆ Impose copayments of about $10 for in-network services, 30 percent for going out of network
◆ Have out-of-pocket maximums for out-of-network expenses; $2,400 for individuals, $4,000 for families
◆ In 1995 cost, on average, $3,415

impose a flat fee, such as $10 per doctor visit; out-of-network copayments run 30 percent or more. Access to specialists is less restricted than in HMOs; most PPOs allow more flexibility to visit a specialist without having preapproval by your primary-care physician.

PPOs have yearly out-of-pocket maximums, averaging $1,200 for individuals using in-network providers, $2,000 for out-of-network care. They also have lifetime payout maximums.

The point-of-service plan: A POS is a hybrid. If you use a health-care provider within your plan's network, it works a lot like an HMO: you pay no deductible and usually only a small copayment of $10 per visit. If you go outside the network, it functions like a PPO: you are subject to a deductible, usually about $300 for an individual and $600 for a family, and a sizable copayment, 30 percent of the physician's charges.

In a POS, as in a PPO, you can mix the types of care you receive, using, for example, a longtime internist who happens not to be in the network and a pediatrician who is. This combination of cost savings and flexibility reassures frugal consumers who don't want to switch from trusted physicians to strangers. As a result, POS plans grew faster in 1993 and '94 than HMOs or PPOs.

THE ABCs OF HMOs

AS MORE AND MORE EMPLOYEES find themselves in managed-care plans, one question nags at consumers' minds: With their strong emphasis on cost containment, can these programs deliver the same high-quality care as traditional fee-for-service plans? The unsatisfying answer to that question is, it depends. As with most products, quality varies from one organization to the next. Unfortunately, comparative information is often lacking or inadequate to help you choose the one best for you. This section tells you what sort of questions you need to answer, and where to find some of the answers.

On average, several studies have shown, patients don't fare any better or worse in HMOs, which are the oldest and best-studied form of managed-care organizations. Outcomes—how often patients are cured or improve, medicine's ultimate report card—are similar for HMOs and private practitioners. But as any statistician will tell you, averages apply to a universe, not individuals or even particular groups. And there is some evidence that certain groups of seriously ill patients—those with AIDS, for instance—may not fare as well in managed care.

On the plus side, HMOs and some other managed-care organizations do tend to provide or cover treatment that traditional plans don't: well-child checkups, immunizations, and annual physicals, for instance. And contrary to what you might think, the doctors who work for managed-care plans aren't the second-tier ones who couldn't make it on their own. "It's a misconception that the doctors who join don't have a practice," says Inlander, of People's Medical Society. "What happens is that managed-care companies and big businesses sit down and review what doctors the employees are already going to in large numbers, and they try to recruit those doctors first. They know their employees don't want to switch doctors." An estimated 77 percent of physicians in the United States have managed-care contracts.

Managed-care executives like to point to opinion surveys showing that 90 percent of people in HMOs are perfectly happy with their care. But, as one expert wryly noted, "most of those people aren't sick and aren't using their HMO much. They should survey sick people and see what they think."

Among those consumers who do use their plans and do have complaints, one of the most common concerns the gatekeeper system, in which it is your primary-care physician, not you, who decides whether you can see a specialist. The gatekeeper concept is common in HMOs and POS plans, less so in PPOs. This procedure, critics say, can make it more difficult for you to get specialized care when you feel you need it.

Probably the most troubling aspect of managed-care firms is the way they pay their physicians. Many have their doctors on salary, while some pay physicians a fee for each service rendered.

Others, however, give each doctor a fixed annual fee for every member patient he or she sees. All costs of care come out of that fee, including appointments, tests, and treatment by specialists. Any overruns come out of the physician's pocket. In another fee arrangement, the managed-care company may pay a bonus to physicians who keep costs low or who don't exceed a quota of specialist referrals and laboratory tests. Most physicians no doubt try to do well by their patients, but built-in incentives to hold back on treatment are disturbing.

Many companies, especially larger ones, offer employees a choice among a few types of health plans, including an indemnity plan and perhaps more than one managed-care organization. Before enrolling in a managed-care plan, you'll want to know its particular pros and cons. So gather all the information you can.

Ask your employer's benefits manager or human resources department for material on the care plans being offered you. They should have it. After all, they're the ones who did the first round of managed-care shopping.

☞ Don't hesitate to go to the managed-care provider itself if you can't get the answers to your questions from your employer.

☞ **Use outside sources of information like the National Committee for Quality Assurance.**

Consumer-friendly, unbiased information about health plans is getting easier to find. NCQA collects information on managed-care plans, including HMOs, rates them on factors such as physician credentials and subscriber turnover, publishes findings, and accredits the plans.

Accreditation means the managed-care company has met fairly strict qualifications. The NCQA makes its reports and accreditation-status list available. At this writing, about half the country's managed-care plans have been reviewed, so lack of accreditation isn't necessarily a black mark; being turned down for accreditation is. For information call the NCQA at 800-839-6487 and request its free Accreditation Status report, or access it via the Internet at http://www.ncqa.org.

Another good source of advice is the Center for the Study of Services, a nonprofit consumer-education group in Washington, D.C. The center publishes *The Consumer's Guide to Health Plans*, which ranks some 250 health plans. Cost is $12; 800-475-7283.

HERE ARE SOME QUESTIONS you should try to answer:

◆ What physicians and hospitals are part of the network? Get a complete listing before you decide to sign on. And make sure you have a range of choices. "If you live in a decent-sized community, I like to see at least three specialists in each field so you have choices," recommends Charles Inlander.

◆ How long has the firm done business in this area? A track record of three years or more is recommended.

◆ How many of the plan's doctors are board-certified? The more the better. You're looking for a percentage that is at least at the 70 percent mark.

◆ What are the plan's physician-turnover rates? People leave an organization for many different reasons, but the effect is the same: disruption. Look for a turnover rate no higher than 5 percent for PPO and POS physicians, 10 percent for staff and salaried HMO docs.

◆ What will the plan provider do if you disagree with your primary physician about treatment? It should have a formal appeals procedure, in which other doctors review your objections to your care.

◆ How carefully does the plan listen to its patients? Some organizations take yearly member surveys, ask for evaluations of specific physicians, and reward doctors who get good reviews.

◆ What is the plan's medical-loss ratio? Despite its confusing name, this ratio will give you some straightforward information on how much the plan spends on patient care, as opposed to administration and overhead. The higher the medical-loss ratio, the better. For example, a survey of HMOs done by *Bloomberg Personal* magazine in 1995 found that Kaiser Foundation Health Plan had a medical-loss ratio of 96.5 percent in 1994, meaning the organization spent 96.5 percent of every dollar on patient care; the lowest rate in the survey was 70.2 percent.

◆ How are physicians in the plan reimbursed? You should know if they're being paid a set yearly fee for your care or a fee every time they see you.

☞ Check with any HMO you're considering about reciprocal care.
If you travel often or regularly spend part of the year in another area of the country—winter in Florida or summer in Maine, for instance—you want to be sure your HMO or managed-care company has an arrangement that will allow you to get treatment from providers at your destination. Otherwise, you could get stuck without a health-care provider when traveling and be eligible only for emergency treatment. Inquire about the plan's arrangements.

EMPLOYER-PROVIDED HEALTH CARE: MAKING THE MOST OF IT

IF YOU WORK FOR A COMPANY that provides you with health insurance, count yourself fortunate. Most employers pick up the lion's share of their employees' premiums, a fringe benefit that's tax-free. (If your company pays the full cost of coverage, you are truly in the privileged minority—enjoy it, but don't count on the arrangement lasting indefinitely.) More important, without that benefit you'd be in the unenviable position of having to buy your own insurance.

In 1995 employers paid an average $3,821 per employee for health insurance. If you had to buy your own, it would cost you far more. Group rates are cheaper than individual rates, and the coverage available to groups tends to be more comprehensive. Moreover, an employer-provided plan won't reject you because of a bad medical history. So consider your company's health insurance an asset, and make the most of it.

The first step is to choose your coverage carefully. Many employers offer more than one health-insurance arrangement: roughly half of all employers now offer two or more managed-care options. Typically, when you start work at a company, you are asked which plan you wish to enroll in; established employees get the chance to change their plans once a year, usually toward year end.

It can be a confusing choice, made even more complex if you have to consider a spouse's coverage and how to coordinate the two plans. A recent survey by pollsters Louis Harris and Associates found that most people want more information than is given in the glossy brochures and indecipherable memos often passed along by the benefits or human resources department. But until that information is forthcoming, you have to make sure you ask the right questions of the right sources yourself. That means looking beyond your paycheck deductions.

"Most employees look at two factors when choosing a plan: the monthly or weekly employee contribution and whether or not their current providers are in a plan," says Allison Kalban-Gernett, a benefits consultant at Apex Management. "But those aren't the only things you should look at. Look at what each plan actually covers."

☞ **If you have a complaint about care, voice it to the plan administrators and doctors, but don't forget to tell your employer, too.**
Your boss, after all, is paying the biggest chunk of the bills and has a lot more leverage with the HMO than you do as an individual. Sometimes an employer can intervene on your behalf if you're having trouble getting satisfaction.

☞ **Compare each plan's coverage with your anticipated health-care needs.**
You'd need a crystal ball to predict all your year's doctor and hospital trips, but some costs you can bet on. If you're planning to get pregnant, see how maternity care is covered. If you have or are planning to have children, look into plan payments for immunizations and children's checkups, also called well-baby care. Check the plan's restrictions on, or exclusions of, specialized care, such as chiropractic or infertility treatments, dental or podiatric care, mental-health and substance-abuse counseling. See how it treats annual physical exams and payments for prescription drugs. Don't pay for more coverage than you think you'll need, but don't leave yourself unprotected, either.

☞ **Check the plans' choices of networked physicians and hospitals. Are your current caregivers listed? Is it important to you?**
Most people covered by employer-sponsored health plans are now enrolled in managed-care programs. But if you have

a long-standing relationship with a trusted physician who isn't part of a PPO or HMO network, you may be willing to pay more to be in a plan that allows at least some reimbursement for out-of-network caregivers. On the other hand, if you don't have a preference in doctors, you may be able to cut your costs by enrolling in a plan that restricts your freedom of choice.

☞ **Compare your out-of-pocket costs—contributions, deductibles, and so on—under each plan.**
Monthly (or weekly) employee contributions are the obvious expenses, but there are others as well. The deductible is one. Should you pay a higher contribution for a lower deductible? If you choose that route and stay healthy, you're paying for coverage you never use.

A helpful calculation is to see how long you'd have to stay healthy before the deductible amount for which you're responsible—but haven't paid—is exceeded by your savings on premiums. For example, if a plan that has a $500 deductible is $50 cheaper per month than one with a $200 deductible, you'd only have to stay healthy for six months to equal the extra $300 you'd pay out of pocket before your benefits kick in.

Coinsurance is another expense to consider. Does the insurer require you to pay 20 or 25 percent of your doctor bills? Is there an out-of-pocket maximum, after which it picks up more of your expenses? One valuable exercise: look at the out-of-pocket costs you would have incurred last year under each of your options.

☞ **Beware: there may be waiting periods for pre-existing conditions.**
When you are simply exercising your yearly right to change your coverage under your employer-sponsored plan, exclusions of preexisting conditions are uncommon and are prohibited in some states. They most often become an issue when you change jobs. If you have such a condition and none of your new job's plans will pay for treatment for a

period, try to extend coverage from your old employer through the use of Cobra (more on that on page 89).

☞ Don't duplicate your spouse's coverage.

This is tricky. If you and your spouse have no children and both your bosses offer health insurance, you may each want to keep your individual coverage. Sometimes employers require only a small (or no) contribution from an employee with no family to cover.

If you have children, however, you might do better opting for one employer's family plan and dropping the other spouse's coverage altogether. That way you won't pay for care already covered under the more comprehensive family plan.

Before you opt out of your employer's health plan, though, find out when and if you can sign back on again should your situation change. You don't want to be left unprotected if your spouse is laid off, for example.

☞ Look for a lifetime maximum benefit of at least $1 million.

If you are in a plan that has a lower maximum, you should ask your benefits department to raise it or see if you can buy add-on catastrophic coverage; since the plan maximum is rarely reached, such an add-on is not especially expensive. In a true catastrophe, even that may not be enough. Actor Christopher Reeve made headlines earlier this year urging Congress to mandate lifetime caps of $10 million. Reeve said he estimates his health-care costs since his tragic riding accident, which has confined him to a wheelchair and respirator, to be $400,000 a year, while his health-policy cap is $1.2 million.

☞ Read the benefits book carefully.

Once you've signed with a plan, pay close attention to its rules and restrictions. I once foolishly overlooked the requirement that the insurance company be contacted within 48 hours of a hospital emergency-room visit. When my son was injured on a playground and had to be transported via ambulance to the local hospital, it didn't occur to me to report it to the company until I received notification that they were not going to pay the hospital bill. After several long phone calls, my insurer finally relented, but you can bet I took another look at the fine print.

The plan descriptions given earlier list other common requirements. A few not already mentioned: Many plans, indemnity as well as managed-care, require that insurers be notified before nonemergency surgery and may demand a second opinion. Some will pay only for admission on the day of surgery, rather than the night before, and for preadmission, rather than in-patient, testing. Insurers also insist that many procedures be done on an out-patient basis.

☞ **Watch out for "usual, customary, and reasonable," or UCR, charges.**
When a plan says it reimburses 80 percent of physicians bills, it means "80 percent of what's reasonable," and your insurer's definition of reasonable may be different from your doctor's. National consulting firms provide insurance companies with statistics about customary fees for particular services in your geographic area. If your doctor charges $2,500 for a procedure but the UCR fee is $2,000, your insurer will pay you only 80 percent of the $2,000; you're responsible for the balance. Protect yourself. When your doctor recommends a procedure, ask how much it costs, then find out what your plan's UCR is for the treatment. If there's a big discrepancy, you may be able to budge your doctor. Use the UCR as ammunition to argue the price down, or ask if he or she will accept your insurance company's payment as full reimbursement. Alternatively, your doctor may be able to provide you with names of insurers that do fully reimburse for the same service. Or you could call a sampling of other physicians and query them about their fees.

☞ **Use flexible-spending accounts.**
Strictly speaking, these are not health-insurance plans. They are another type of employer-provided health benefit that allows you to pay for care with untaxed dollars. This is the

way it works: You estimate your medical expenses—including your deductible and items not covered by your health plan, such as eyeglasses—for the coming year. You then have your employer deduct that amount, in equal installments, from your wages each pay period and set it aside in an account. When you incur an eligible expense, you pay the bill and are reimbursed from these reserved funds.

The kicker is the tax benefit. Money put into a flex account is not subject to federal or state taxes (except currently, for some reason, New Jersey and Pennsylvania taxes). Your savings can be impressive: if you were in a 35 percent tax bracket and had $1,000 in medical bills to pay, you'd come out $350 ahead paying through a flex account. The drawback is that you have to spend all the money in the account during the plan year. If your actual medical expenses turn out to be less than you anticipated and you finish up the year with money in your account, you forfeit it to your employer. So as the end of the plan year approaches, make sure you find ways to spend your balance: get a physical exam, buy new eyeglasses, or stock up on contact-lens solution.

🖝 Beware the MEWA.

If you work for a small company, your employer may be insuring you through a multiemployer welfare arrangement. A MEWA administers the health plans of a group of small member companies, using the combined premiums to provide coverage. Generally, MEWAs self-insure, though some buy coverage from established insurance companies. Often employers find that this arrangement saves them money on their health-insurance premiums.

There are good MEWAs; however, in recent years, some have defrauded customers. At its worst, a MEWA collects premiums and pays small claims at first but gradually siphons money into the pockets of its operators. When big medical claims come in, the MEWA closes down, leaving employees with no coverage, big bills, and preexisting conditions that will hinder their chances of getting new health coverage. The General Accounting Office reported that in the three-and-a-half-year period ending in mid-1991, MEWAs had left $123 million in unpaid claims for nearly 400,000 workers in the United States.

To protect yourself against MEWA fraud or incompetence, ask some basic questions early on. Find out what business experience the MEWA's administrators have and who is providing the insurance, and request a copy of the organization's audited financial statements. Find out from your state insurance department if the MEWA is licensed to do business in your state and if there have been complaints about it. Also, be sure the insurer, if the MEWA contracts with one, participates in a state guarantee fund, which can help pay claims a MEWA doesn't. If you find that your employer is using a shaky MEWA, you may want to lobby to switch or consider buying your own health insurance.

COBRA: BUYING TIME FOR YOURSELF AND YOUR FAMILY

IN THESE TIMES OF UNSETTLED employment, you could well lose your job, and with it your coverage. If you do, your first step should probably be to exploit Cobra.

The Consolidated Omnibus Budget Reconciliation Act of 1985 was an obscure federal budget bill. Attached to it, however, was a very important provision for insurance consumers. According to this provision, if you quit your job or have your hours reduced, or if you are fired (unless the reason is gross misconduct), your employer must offer you and your dependents continued coverage. You have to pay the full premium plus a bit—102 percent of the company's annual group premium—but you can't be turned down because of bad health. And you will get the same coverage you had immediately before becoming eligible for Cobra, extending it up to 18 months for you and up to 36 months for your dependents. Cobra also applies to spouses and children who would otherwise lose coverage because of divorce, or the worker's death, or when the worker becomes eligible for Medicare.

So if you have been laid off or have recently been divorced or widowed by a plan-covered spouse and would otherwise be without health insurance, the best place to turn initially is your (or your ex's) ex-employer. The coverage isn't indefinite, but it gives you a chance to get your bearings and shop for individual coverage, or to find another employer who offers health benefits. Don't delay doing the paperwork: you must sign up for Cobra within 60 days of receiving notice from your employer.

HOW TO BUY YOUR OWN COVERAGE

IT'S A COLD, CRUEL WORLD out there when you're buying your own health insurance. Prices are high, coverage can be hard to find, and benefits may be limited.

Ask Judah Holstein, a Westchester County, New York, computer-software consultant. When Holstein left a large consulting firm to start his own business, he knew he'd have to shop long and hard for a decent health-insurance policy to cover him and his wife. As a first step, he decided to continue coverage with his former employer under a Cobra plan. For 18 months, Holstein and his wife were covered by the POS plan they had previously been enrolled in, which allowed them to use the out-of-network physicians they preferred. For that privilege, their annual deductible was $700, and their copayment was 30 percent for out-of-network doctors. Their monthly payment was about $450, below what it would have been on the open market, since their rates were still figured as part of the employee group.

When the 18 months were up, Holstein went shopping for an individual policy. His ex-employer's insurer, a division of Prudential, offered him and his wife a conversion policy, but Holstein never seriously considered it. "It had a $3,000 deductible and didn't cover much," he says.

Instead, Holstein went with an indemnity plan sold through an association for self-employed people that he had joined. But he ended up being disappointed with the coverage. When the couple's son was born, they had to pay nearly $3,000 out of their own pockets for charges associated with the pregnancy and delivery that the plan didn't cover.

So Holstein went insurance shopping again. He shrewdly contacted professional organizations he was qualified to join: a computer-professionals group and an engineering association. He also queried the local managed-care companies. Ultimately, he opted for one of the latter. Since he had last looked at plans two years earlier, the couple's trusted pediatrician, obstetrician-gynecologist, and general practitioner had signed up with Oxford, a managed-care firm in their area. Though the plan assesses stiff penalties for going out-of-network, including a $2,500 deductible before anything is covered, the Holsteins don't anticipate needing to do so. Other plans offered no out-of-network coverage at all.

"For us, the key to happiness is that our doctors were in the plan," says Holstein. The family's premium is $546 a month, or $6,552 a year.

Whether you willingly leave the corporate cocoon, like the Holsteins, or are laid off, or work for one of the increasing number of businesses that have no health-insurance benefits (about 56 percent of people without health insurance work for firms that don't offer it, according to the Employee Benefits Research Institute), you could easily find yourself without employer-provided coverage. Given the hassle and expense of enrolling in individual policies, you may be tempted to go without, rationalizing that you're healthy or that you can't possibly afford it. Don't try it. And don't bargain with yourself that it will only be for a few months, until you find a job with benefits; get a short-term policy if you genuinely

think your need is short term—if you're a newly mint-
ed college grad, for example. Probably nothing can
decimate a family's assets faster than an uninsured
health crisis. And if you wait until you're sick to get
insurance, it's going to be unobtainable or prohibitively expensive.

If you've left a job where you had insurance benefits, follow Holstein's lead and take advantage of
Cobra. When this coverage runs out, you can often
get a conversion policy from the Cobra insurer, but as
Holstein found out, these are notoriously expensive—
even more so than ordinary individual health policies.
That's because conversion plans can't reject applicants based on medical problems, so they charge
higher premiums. If your health is bad, a conversion
policy may be your best bet. But if you're reasonably
healthy, you should be able to get more extensive coverage elsewhere at a lower price.

You can probably find the lowest prices with an
HMO, PPO, or POS; the tips on choosing an individual managed-care plan are much the same as those
given earlier for group plans. But if you're intent on
enrolling in a traditional indemnity plan, here are
guidelines on what to look for:

◆ Insurance that can't be yanked away from you.
Guaranteed renewable is the term for you want. That
means the insurer can't discontinue your coverage
if you become ill. Premiums may go up as you get
older, but they will rise for all the company's policies, not just yours.

◆ A financially stable insurer. It doesn't do you any
good to have guaranteed-renewable coverage if the
company providing it goes belly-up. Look for an
insurer with a rating of A or A+ from ratings companies such as A.M. Best, Standard & Poor's Corp.,
Moody's Investors Service, Duff & Phelps, and
Weiss. (Telephone numbers for these firms can be
found in "Resources," page 224.)

◆ A policy that will cover preexisting conditions. But be forewarned: many individual policies do impose a waiting period before covering treatment for a preexisting condition. The shorter the period the better. Some companies make you wait three months; others a year. (During the waiting period, treatment for other conditions is covered.) Anything more than a year is unacceptable.

◆ Major-medical, rather than hospital-surgical, coverage. Hospital-surgical policies cover only hospital services and surgical procedures. You want a major-medical policy that takes care of all hospital costs, including room, emergency-room treatment, nursing care, anesthesia, tests and X rays, and drugs. Make certain, too, that outpatient, or same-day, surgery is covered. Surgeries that are truly elective—a face-lift, for example—are rarely covered by anyone.

◆ At least partial coverage for these other medical services: physician bills, skilled nursing-home care for recovery and rehabilitation periods, prescription drugs, medical equipment and supplies such as oxygen, and home health care.

◆ A policy that protects you against the expenses of catastrophic illness. Look for a lifetime maximum payout of at least $1 million and an annual out-of-pocket maximum, which places a limit on what you have to spend in any one year. What your maximum should be is a personal matter (how much can you afford to pay?), but amounts of a few thousand dollars, after the deductible is paid, are probably manageable.

◆ A waiver-of-premium provision, which lets you skip paying insurance premiums if you're ill or injured.

◆ The highest deductible (at least $1,000) and copayment (at least 20 percent of costs) you can afford. You can bet that insurance with a low deductible comes with a high price tag. High copayments also reduce premiums. And if you have a decent out-of-pocket maximum, you don't have to worry about medical-care costs getting out of hand.

👉 **Don't waste your money on single-disease coverage or hospital indemnity insurance.**
Insurers prey on the very real fears people have of contracting specific ailments, such as cancer. But you need comprehensive health insurance that will provide care no matter what the cause of illness is.

Accident-only insurance is similar to single-disease coverage, paying if you lose a limb or your sight, or perhaps covering medical care only in the event of an accident, not an illness. Again, comprehensive health insurance is the order of the day.

Hospital indemnity insurance is what you see advertised on daytime or late-night television with promises to pay $100 a day if you're hospitalized. These policies have a couple of problems. First, though more and more treatment, including expensive surgical procedures, is being done on an outpatient basis, the policies usually exclude this type of care. Second, with the average daily cost of hospitalization hovering around $820, the $100-a-day payout will leave you with big hospital bills.

Credit accident and sickness insurance is another type of coverage you shouldn't buy. This is pitched to you when you take out a loan to buy something, such as an automobile or appliances, and is designed to cover the monthly loan payment if you become totally disabled. It's a lousy idea; debts and financial obligations are better covered through a general disability policy. (See "Disability Insurance," page 112.)

HOW TO FIND COVERAGE
IF YOU'RE HARD TO INSURE

OF ALL THE SAD IRONIES in the health-insurance system, none seems more unfair than this: if you have had medical problems and really need insurance, nobody wants to sell it to you. If you've been diagnosed with cancer (even if the disease is in remission), if you have a history of heart attacks or hypertension, diabetes, epilepsy, or a number of other conditions, individual coverage can be tough to find. Insurers pay special attention to conditions treated in the past five years, although some go back further.

Also, people in certain professions may be turned down for individual coverage. Some, such as pro athletes and race-car drivers, perform physically dangerous jobs. Others just belong to groups that insurance companies believe file a lot of claims—lawyers and doctors, for instance.

If you are having difficulty finding health insurance, here are some tips:

- Try the Blue Cross/Blue Shield organization in your area. Some are required by law to have open-enrollment periods when they must accept new subscribers regardless of medical history.

- Call local HMOs. Some of those also have open-enrollment periods.

- Contact your state insurance department. As of 1995, 23 states had high-risk health-insurance pools to cover otherwise-uninsurable residents. Other states allow insurance companies to sell bare-bones policies to customers they consider problematic. These policies offer basic coverage and may require higher deductibles and copayments. Be sure you understand exactly what such a plan covers. Many offer reduced benefits for certain conditions, such as mental and nervous conditions and organ transplants. They aren't ideal, but they're better than nothing.

- Try to hook up with any group or association you can—a professional group, a college alumni group, whatever. Any way that you can piggyback on a group rate will help.

- Don't be tempted to fudge health conditions on your application. And don't do business with any agent who suggests that you do. First of all, you're unlikely to get away with it. If you've sought medical treatment for a condition, the information is probably on file at the Medical Information Bureau. MIB is a huge clearinghouse of data that insurers use in deciding whether to sell you a policy and what to charge you if they do (sort of like the IRS, only it keeps track of your health, not your wealth). And if you do manage to get a policy based on a fudged application, when you get sick, the insurance company will no doubt try to avoid paying your claim.

◆ Check your MIB file. If you think you've been denied coverage unfairly, the culprit could be an error in your medical history. The bureau is required to provide rejected applicants with copies of their files. You may spot inaccuracies that you and your doctor can effectively rebut. The MIB can be reached at 617-426-3660.

INSURING THE GOLDEN YEARS

WHEN YOU REACH AGE 65, you might think your insurance problems are solved. After all, you're now eligible for Medicare. In the 30 years since Lyndon Johnson signed the federal health-insurance program for the elderly and disabled into law, it has become a senior citizen's best friend, making coverage available to millions who would otherwise be unable to afford it and keeping the elderly from being bankrupted by illness. But Medicare is no panacea. It doesn't pay for everything. Figuring out just what is covered, and how fully, can be a bureaucratic brainteaser. It's worth the effort, though: once you know where the holes are, you may decide you need to plug them with a medigap or long-term-care policy or with some other supplemental programs.

The first thing to understand is that Medicare is not Medicaid. Medicaid is a state-administered program, financed with both state and federal funds, that pays for health care for the poor regardless of age (including, as explained below, nursing-home care for seniors with minimal assets); Medicare is federally administered and covers those over 65, regardless of income. Medicaid requires no contributions from its beneficiaries; Medicare is a true insurance program, whose premiums are paid out of taxes or deducted from your monthly Social Security check.

Together, the two programs have made the federal government the country's largest health insurer. Not surprisingly, then, they are being scrutinized on Capitol Hill. Democrats and Republicans agree that they must rein in the programs' ballooning costs to have any realistic chance of controlling the federal deficit. At this writing, legislation is being debated that would raise fees for retirees and cut coverage, but it is anybody's guess whether it will find its way into the law books.

Whether those particular measures are put into effect or not, you can bet on change of some kind. Make sure you aren't caught by surprise. Probably the best way to keep up to date on Medicare is to get a copy of the most recent Medicare Handbook, put out by the Health Care Financing Administration, which details coverage and fees. You automatically get a copy of this booklet the first year you register for Medicare; after that you have to request it. Ask your local Social Security office or write to the U.S. Dept. of Health and Human Services, Health Care Financing Administration, 6323 Security Blvd., Baltimore, MD 21207-5187.

MEDICARE

IN THE MEANTIME, here's the way Medicare works now. The program consists of two parts. Part A pays for hospital treatment, as well as for limited stays in skilled nursing homes and hospices and some home health care. You're automatically eligible for Part A when you reach 65. The premiums are paid out of tax dollars. So you owe nothing, as long as you qualify for Social Security. If you don't qualify, you can pay the premiums when you reach age 65 and buy into the system yourself. Contact your local Social Security office for details.

Part B of Medicare pays for items and services that Part A doesn't cover, such as physician visits, outpatient surgery, X rays and laboratory tests, and some medical supplies and pharmaceuticals. It is optional and will cost you extra. When you register for Part A, you'll be asked if you want to participate in Part B. If you say yes, the premium will usually be deducted from your Social Security check. The amount increases yearly, but for 1996 it is $42.50 a month. That's if you sign up within six months of turning 65 (or within six months of becoming eligible for Medicare); if you wait longer, the monthly premiums are higher.

MEDICARE: WHAT YOU PAY IN 1996

Medicare Part A Premium:
  For senior citizens who qualify for Social Security = 0
  For seniors who don't qualify = $289 a month

Part A Deductible: $736

Part A Daily Copayment of Hospitalization Costs:
  Days 1 through 60 in a benefit period = 0
  Days 61 through 90 = $184
  Lifetime reserve days = $368

Part A Daily Copayment of Extended Care Days in a SNF (skilled nursing facility):
  Days 1 through 20 in a benefit period = 0
  Days 21 through 100 = $92 per day

Medicare Part B Premium: $42.50 a month

Medicare Part B Deductible: $100

Just about the only time you shouldn't sign up for Part B is if you're still working and covered by an employee health plan. Don't rely on a retiree health plan that may be provided by the company you retired from to replace Part B coverage. Many such plans specifically exclude costs that are covered by Medicare.

Even if you've signed up for both Part A and B, though, you're still going to be hit by cost sharing, deductibles, and gaps in coverage. In fact, despite its rising costs, Medicare pays for less than half the health-care expenses incurred by older Americans. To understand what is and isn't covered, you need to come to terms with "benefit periods."

The benefit period is a concept only a bureaucrat could have devised. A period begins when you are admitted to a hospital and ends once you've been out of the hospital, or a skilled nursing facility (SNF) to which you were discharged for rehab, for 60 consecutive days. So if you're hospitalized for 10 days, then are discharged, then a week later are hospitalized again, both hospital stays take place in the same benefit period.

Part A pays for 90 days of hospitalization during each benefit period. It covers the entire cost of eligible care for up to 60 days. After that, you're subject to a copayment. If you are hospitalized more than 90 days, you can draw on a lifetime maximum of 60 reserve days. For each reserve day you use, you're liable for a copayment. After the reserve days are depleted, you pay the whole cost of your hospitalization. Fortunately, very few people stay in a hospital more than 60 days; fewer still use up their lifetime reserve.

Every year the amount of the deductibles, premiums, and copayments you owe is adjusted for inflation. The box at left lists the figures for 1996.

WHAT UNCLE SAM WILL
AND WON'T PAY FOR

MEDICARE WILL PAY MOST of your hospital costs, once a hospital-utilization-review administrator has determined you're not being hospitalized when outpatient treatment would do as well. Among the uncovered items are many that traditional health-insurance policies won't pay for either: private rooms, unless they are medically necessary, and convenience items, like a telephone or television. The list below highlights some of the important expenses that Parts A and B will and will not cover. In addition, of course, deductibles and copayments are built into both parts.

Covered: Eighty percent of reasonable and customary doctor's bills and 80 percent of the cost of outpatient procedures performed in a hospital.
Not covered: Routine physical examinations, immunizations, and exams to prescribe hearing aids or eyeglasses.

As a general rule, Medicare does not cover anything that could be considered routine care but will pay 80 percent of the cost of treatments for diagnosed medical conditions. This includes chiropractic, optometric, and podiatric treatments.

Covered: Temporary treatment in a skilled nursing facility, up to 100 days per benefit period.
Not covered: Long-term nursing-home care.

SNF coverage has several requirements. A few: you must have been in the hospital for at least three days before being discharged to a nursing home, and a medical professional must certify that you require skilled nursing or rehabilitative services on a daily basis.

Covered: Inpatient care at a psychiatric hospital for a lifetime maximum of 190 days. Also 50 percent of the cost of treatment from a psychiatrist, up to a maximum of $1,100 a year.

Not covered: More than the 190 days of inpatient psychiatric treatment, regardless of when you received them or your medical condition; treatment by psychologists or social workers that have not been specifically approved by Medicare.

Covered: Medications administered by injection, whether in a hospital or not.

Not covered: Other prescription medications.

☞ **Ask if your doctor "accepts assignment."**

Doctors are allowed by law to charge you up to 115 percent of the Medicare-allowed fee for a given procedure. However, if your doctor accepts assignment, he or she has agreed to take whatever Medicare pays as full payment. In that case, you should never owe a balance beyond the standard 20 percent copayment.

MEDIGAP: PLUGGING THE HOLES

BETWEEN DEDUCTIBLES, copayments, lifetime and benefit-period limits, and uncovered items and services, Medicare leaves you liable for a lot of medical costs. To make up the difference, about half of the people on Medicare have turned to medigap policies.

Not too long ago, the medigap field was a scam artist's dream. It was not unusual to find an elderly patient paying premiums on several policies with overlapping coverage. Plans were just different enough to make comparison shopping almost impossible.

Fortunately, some basic consumer-protection laws are now in effect. Insurance companies are required to offer six months of open enrollment, starting when you reach 65 or first become eligible for Medicare, during which time they can't turn you down for health reasons. After that, poor health can be grounds for rejection, though some companies also have open-

10 MEDIGAP PLANS TO CHOOSE FROM

Since 1992 all medigap policies sold have had to match one of 10 standard benefits plans, labeled A through J. Though not all policies are available in all states and not all insurers offer the full range of policies (they're required to offer Plan A, the basic-benefits plan, but the availability of other plans varies from company to company), the standardization has made comparison shopping easier for seniors.

Basic Benefits: Pays the $184 per day copayment for hospital days 61–90 per benefit period, $368 for days 91–150, and all charges for an extra 365 days in hospital over your lifetime. Pays 20 percent copayment for doctor bills; pays for first three pints of blood yearly.

Part A (Hospital) Deductible: Pays $736 deductible.

Skilled Nursing Home Copayment: Pays $92 per day for days 21–100 in nursing home.

Part B (Doctor) Deductible: Pays $100 deductible for medical services.

Foreign Travel Emergency: Pays for medically necessary emergency care that begins in the first two months of each trip outside the U.S. After a $250 deductible, plan pays 80 percent of expenses when you are away less than three months. Lifetime limit is $50,000.

MEDICARE-SUPPLEMENTAL INSURANCE PLANS

Basic Benefits
Part A (Hospital) Deductible
Skilled Nursing Home Copayment
Part B (Doctor) Deductible
Foreign Travel Emergency
At-Home Recovery
Excess Doctor Charges
Preventative Screening
Outpatient Prescription Drugs

At-Home Recovery: Pays up to $40 per visit (annual maximum $1,600) for no more than seven visits weekly for personal-care services when you also require Medicare-approved skilled home health care. Personal care must be doctor-ordered and can be used for up to eight weeks after Medicare visits stop.

Excess Doctor Charges: Pays difference between doctor's actual charges and Medicare-approved amount. Federal law prohibits doctors from charging more than 115 percent of Medicare-approved amount. Benefit pays either 80 percent or 100 percent of excess fees for services approved by Medicare.

Preventative Screening: Pays up to $120 a year for doctor-ordered health-care screening and preventative services not covered by Medicare.

Outpatient Prescription Drugs: Provides either basic (B) or extended (E) coverage. Basic coverage has $250 per year deductible, pays 50 percent of drugs up to $1,250 annually. Extended has $250 per year deductible and pays 50 percent of drugs up to $3,000. To get the maximum benefit under basic and extended coverage, your prescription costs would have to exceed $2,750 and $6,250, respectively, each year.

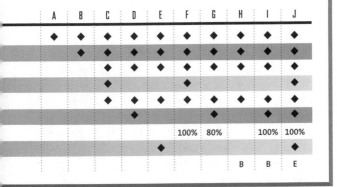

SOURCE: UNITED SENIORS HEALTH COOPERATIVE

enrollment periods once a year. Once you're accepted, policies are guaranteed renewable for life.

Some plans are community-rated. That means that all subscribers in a given geographic area are charged the same premium, regardless of age. Other plans charge older or sicker subscribers more.

Perhaps most important, though, is that all medigap policies must now fall into one of 10 standardized categories, dubbed plans A through J. This makes it far easier for you to compare the coverage and premiums of competing companies.

All the plans provide certain basic benefits: coverage of the Medicare hospital copayment and deductible, as well as 100 percent of the cost for up to 365 additional days of hospitalization per lifetime. Other features vary. Some plans pay excess doctor charges; some cover outpatient prescription drugs and foreign-travel emergencies, which are not covered by Medicare. Generally, plan A is the most barebones and least expensive; J is the Cadillac of coverage. The midrange policies, C through F, are the most popular. The chart on page 102 shows which plans offer which features.

The average premiums for the most basic plan sold run about $50 a month; the J-policy premiums average about $150 a month. Unfortunately, rates for medigap insurance are on the way up. In 1996 policy premiums rose as much as 30 percent.

So, should you buy a medigap policy? It depends. If your income and assets are low enough to qualify for Medicaid, private medigap insurance is probably not affordable and definitely not worth it. Medicaid already takes care of most health-care expenses. If you aren't eligible for Medicaid but still have limited assets, other government-subsidized programs might help you with your health-care costs. Qualified Medicare Beneficiary, QMB, pays the Medicare deductible and Part B premium for participants.

And if you have a slightly higher income, Specified Low-Income Medicare Beneficiaries, SLMB, will pay your Part B premiums. Your local Medicaid office can help you determine if you're eligible for any of these programs.

If you earn too much income to qualify for government assistance, though, you should look into medigap insurance. That goes even if you're covered by your company's retiree health-insurance plan. Many companies are cutting back on retiree benefits or are charging significantly more for them.

And don't stop there. In addition to medigap plans, there are Medicare HMOs and Select polices that can help you reduce medical costs not covered by Medicare.

DECIPHERING THE MEDICARE HMO PITCH

IF YOU HAVEN'T YET HEARD about these, you will. Managed care has swept the under-65 health-insurance market, and the cost of medical care dictates that it will play a big part in Medicare coverage, too. Right now about 10 percent of the 37 million Medicare subscribers use HMOs. This is how it works: You enroll in an HMO that has a Medicare program, and it provides all your care. Social Security pays the premium for Part A directly to the HMO, and your Part B premium also goes to the company.

The basic hospitalization coverage is the same. The advantage is that your other costs are significantly reduced. Typically, there is no deductible for hospital stays, and your copayments are $5 to $15, instead of 20 percent. Many HMOs also cover items and treatments that Medicare doesn't, such as routine exams, prescription drugs, eyeglasses, and dental care. For these benefits, you may have to pay a monthly fee that is similar to a medigap premium. Medicare HMOs have the same disadvantages as any managed-care

plan: Your choice of doctors and physicians is restrict-
ed, and some HMOs have payment arrangements that
give doctors an incentive to limit or deny care. In
addition, your primary-care physician is the one who
decides when and if you need to use specialists.

The AARP (American Association of Retired Persons) is currently studying Medicare HMOs with the
intention of licensing its name to some organizations.
When it does, the group's imprimatur will give
Medicare HMOs a tremendous boost in visibility and
credibility.

☛ **It bears repeating that if you travel widely in your
retirement, or spend part of the year away from home, you
should check what arrangement your Medicare HMO has
made for you to receive routine care.**

☛ **Wait before you drop an existing medigap policy.**
Once you've dropped medigap, it can be tough to reclaim
coverage if you have had health problems. "Give yourself a
chance to test out the HMO," suggests Priscilla Itscoitz, the
manager of the health-insurance counseling program at
United Seniors Health Cooperative. "You want to keep your
options open. You want to keep it until you have some indi-
cation that you're comfortable in the HMO, that they treat
you well, and that you have access to the care you need and
that it is of good quality."

MEDICARE SELECT POLICIES

MEDICARE SELECT IS A SENIOR-CITIZEN variation on
managed care, and is designed to be used instead of a
traditional medigap policy. They work like PPOs.
According to the USHC, Medicare Select policies,
which were originally introduced in 1994 in fifteen
states, may now be sold in all fifty states.

The plans are required to meet the same federal
and state standards as medigap policies and offer
essentially the same coverage, but for premiums that

are 10 to 25 percent lower. As in regular PPOs, patients can go out of network, but they then have to assume a higher percentage of the cost. While Medicare still pays its share of approved charges, if you don't use the network providers, the Medicare Select policy may not pay. So far, coverage for the majority of Medicare Select subscribers has come from Blue Cross/Blue Shield plans.

INSURING FOR
LONG-TERM CARE

YOU MAY HAVE HEARD the frightening statistics: a 65-year-old has at least a 40 percent chance of spending time in a nursing home in his or her lifetime, and the stay there can cost a king's ransom: $30,000 to $70,000 a year. Unless they take precautions—transferring assets to qualify for Medicaid or taking out special insurance, for example—many patients could easily run through their own savings and those of their children.

The problem is that Medicare, which pays for short-term nursing-home stays that are medically necessary, isn't intended to meet long-term custodial needs. And medigap policies and Medicare HMO and Select plans are designed to help pay deductibles and copayments, not to cover custodial care.

That leaves Medicaid, which picks up the tab for about half the nursing-home care in the United States. The catch is that to qualify for Medicaid, you have to be "indigent." The definition of this varies from state to state, but there are a few constants: You can own a house, some personal jewelry (notably, wedding and engagement rings), a car, a term life insurance policy, a prepaid funeral, and a modest amount of cash. That's about it. No stock portfolio. No cache of certificates of deposit or savings accounts. In addition, your monthly income has to be less than the cost of local nursing homes; in some states it can't be more than $1,000 or $1,500 a month.

If your assets amount to more than that, you have to deplete them before Medicaid will kick in. The money doesn't all have to go toward nursing-home bills. Instead, you can "spend down" your assets by giving them to your children or placing them in intricately constructed trusts. But the government doesn't make this easy. And with good reason: Medicaid, after all, was not designed to help upper-middle-class people leave larger inheritances to their children.

First, Medicaid imposes a waiting period after an asset transfer before it will start paying your bills. The length of the period is the number of months of nursing-home care—computed at the average cost for your state—that the assets would have covered, up to a maximum of 36 months or, for some kinds of trusts, five years. Second, you are prohibited from being the direct or indirect beneficiary of the trust, and after you die, Medicaid is authorized to file liens against your estate to try to recoup some of what it paid out during your nursing-home stay.

If you don't want to worry about effecting a transfer early enough to get Medicaid coverage without a waiting a period, or if you want to be able to pay your own way in a nursing home, you might consider long-term-care insurance. Policies vary, but most will pay a specific dollar amount of benefits for each day of care received: $50 or $100 a day, for instance. Benefits extend anywhere from two or three years up to a lifetime. The longer the benefit period, the more expensive the policy. And, as with other types of policies there is a waiting period before benefits kick in, whose length consumers must choose.

Long-term insurance has become more popular in recent years. From 1987 through 1993, the number of individual policies sold grew an average of 27 percent a year; between 1988 and 1993, policies sold through employers mushroomed an average of 88 percent a year. Still, a small percentage of seniors are covered; the AARP estimates that only about 4 percent of people over the age of 65 have long-term-care coverage.

Some states are making it more attractive by participating in a program called Partnership for Long Term Care. This program, now in effect in California, Connecticut, Indiana, and New York, allows consumers who buy long-term-care insurance to apply for Medicaid under special rules when their insurance runs out and so keep more of their assets. Other states are setting up similiar programs.

Long-term-care insurance isn't for everyone. If you're younger than 60, feel free to turn the page and skip to the next chapter. True, the younger you are when you buy long-term-care insurance, the lower the annual premiums are: a 79-year-old would pay a premium of $4,372 a year for a policy that provides benefits of $100 a day for nursing-home care and $50 a day for home health care for a period of four years, while a 50-year-old would only pay $405 annually for the same coverage.

But don't let an agent use that pitch to convince you if you're 50 years old. Unless you have a family history of early-onset Alzheimers disease or some other reason to believe you will need nursing-home care before you reach old age, there are too many unknowns. You'll be paying for benefits that you probably won't need for a couple of decades, and who knows what health care and nursing-home care in America is going to look like—and cost—then? Will the benefit reimbursement levels you've chosen be adequate? Will your insurance company still be in business?

If you have limited financial assets, the policies are just too expensive. Nobody should spend more than 5 to 10 percent of his income on the monthly premium.

If you're rich, skip it. You can afford to pay out of your own pocket. If your net worth is more like

$250,000 to $1 million, though, you might be a candidate for long-term-care insurance.

REMEMBER:

◆ Once you buy a policy, don't stop paying the premium. If you do, not only aren't you covered in most cases, but you forfeit everything you've already paid.

◆ Make sure the policy is guaranteed renewable for life. Otherwise, the insurer could cancel when it looks like you may actually use the benefits.

◆ Check that it will let a physician decide if you need long-term care. Some policies pay only for nursing-home stays that occur immediately after discharge from a hospital, but most long-term stays don't fall into that category.

◆ Look for a policy with level premiums. This means that the company can't lure you in with a low rate and then hike it dramatically after you've signed on. It can still raise its premium if costs go up, but not because of your age: if you buy a policy when you're 55, for instance, you'll always pay the premiums that a current 55-year-old would pay, even when you're actually 75.

◆ Insist on an inflation clause that boosts how much the insurer will pay as nursing-home costs climb. They have most certainly risen in the past 15 years, and there's every reason to think they'll continue to climb precipitously over the next decade or two.

◆ Ask for a provision waiving premiums once you're in a home. If you're a patient in a nursing home, the last thing you need to worry about is premiums.

◆ Look for a policy that provides for home health care. Most older people prefer to remain in their own homes, if possible.

◆ Try to get "protection from lapse." This may provide for third-party notification in case of a missed premium payment, or reinstatement if there is proof that the lapse was due to a cognitive impairment on the part of the insured.

◆ Make sure the policy covers cognitive impairments such as Alzheimers, when a patient may be otherwise physically healthy but still need long-term care, and any illnesses or conditions you may already have when it is issued.

◆ Insist on a financial rating of A or A+ or the equivalent from the rating agencies that monitor the financial stability of insurance companies. (See "Resources," page 224, or "Agencies and Their Ratings," page 146, for ratings information.)

◆ Buy coverage for three years with a daily payment of at least $110, pegged to the national average cost of nursing-home care. The average nursing-home stay is less than three years, and lifetime benefits are much more expensive.

◆ Turn to your local agency on aging and your state insurance department for help in understanding and comparing specific policies.

◆ Find out if your employer offers long-term-care plans. Coverage may be available not only for you, but for parents and other family members.

CHAPTER

4

Disability
INSURANCE

Protecting Your Income

YOUR MOST IMPORTANT financial asset probably isn't your home, your car, or your mutual-fund collection. It is your ability to earn a living. Of all the horror stories agents hear, the saddest ones are from people who are left destitute after an accident because they cannot work and had no coverage, insufficient coverage, or coverage that ran out after a short time.

Unless you're the lucky recipient of a hefty inheritance or can live off your large investment portfolio, you, like most of us, probably need a paycheck. So ask yourself a simple question: how long could you pay your bills and continue your current lifestyle if you were sick or injured for an extended period and couldn't work? Disability insurance is designed to pay you an income if you're too sick to earn one. This chapter will tell you how to get enough insurance for your needs

and how to get it at a reasonable cost.

Think you're unlikely to get so sick that you can't work? Consider the experience of Marilyn MacGruder Barnewall. A former bank vice-president, Barnewall started a bank-consulting company in 1979. Within a few years she had built her business to the point where, at age 46, she was earning about $200,000 a year and advising banks in Europe, Asia, and the United States on how to set up private banking departments. In 1989 what had been a mild case of osteoarthritis became a fullblown case. The anti-inflammatory medicine that had provided relief needed to be increased but began to cause stomach bleeding and additional pain. A bone scan indicated that the arthritis was spreading to Barnewall's thoracic spine region, her ankles, and hips. She couldn't bend, lift, walk, or stand in one place for an extended period.

Although she couldn't continue working as a consultant, Barnewall decided to establish a new career as an author, since she had already written technical books on banking. But within six months she had developed problems with the optic nerve in her left eye that caused depth-perception deficiencies and violent headaches if she spent much time in front of a computer screen. So much for her career change. Luckily, 10 years earlier, as a single mother of two, she'd had the foresight to buy a disability-insurance policy, which cost her $2,000 a year. In 1993 she applied for benefits, was approved, and will collect a "paycheck" of about $20,000 a year until she is 65—or a total of $220,000 for a premium outlay of $22,000. "I shudder to think about what would have become of me without it," says Barnewall.

☞ If you don't have any disability coverage, get it, get it, get it.

Disability insurance is one of the most frequent gaps in a family's finances. Fewer than 25 percent of all American workers have long-term disability coverage. Why? For one thing, it's relatively expensive, even for fairly modest benefits. And no one thinks that disaster will befall him. The premiums for a policy replacing $50,000 of income a year can easily run $2,000 a year—no small sum, especially for young workers. Weighed against the possible financial calamity, though, it makes sense for most unprotected families.

The rise in two-income families in recent years may plug the disability gap a bit—if one member was disabled, the other would provide some income. But most two-income families have expenses that require two incomes. There are frightening statistics out there about disability, and you may have seen them, perhaps from an insurance agent trying to sell you coverage. The most frequently cited one goes something like this: more than 50 percent of 25-year-olds will have sustained a disability lasting 90 days or more by the time they reach the age of 65. True, these statistics take into account all occupations, including those that have higher risks of injury, such as factory and construction jobs. Typical white-collar workers face a much smaller risk—about 4 percent—of suffering such a disability. But even a 4 percent chance is plenty high enough to warrant insurance, particularly when your family could face financial ruin.

☞ **Like life insurance, disability coverage is best bought when you're healthy.**
Another reason to buy disability even if you have some coverage through your employer: you can be rejected if you have a damning medical history. If the only insurance you have is with your employer, you'd better hope the company doesn't drop it, or that if you switch jobs, your new employer also has coverage. Group disability through your employer doesn't travel with you.

☞ **If you have group disability coverage through your employer, give your policy a thorough checkup.**
You may want to buy supplemental disability insurance. Many people mistakenly believe they have adequate coverage from their workplace. But recent employee-benefit surveys show this isn't necessarily true, especially if your employer is a smaller company. Less than 20 percent of companies with fewer than 100 employees offer long-term disability coverage. Even in companies that do offer long-term coverage, the policy may not be comprehensive. Many company policies limit the number of years that disability payments will continue to perhaps two to five years. And for high-income executives, the benefits may be limited to a small percentage of their salary.

☞ **Check out government disability coverage at the federal and state level.**

Government-administered worker's compensation will cover you for injuries that occur on the job. For example, a factory worker injured while operating a piece of equipment would be eligible for worker's comp. Since each state's regulations are different, how much workers receive in benefits varies widely and depends on their earnings and, in some cases, the number of dependents they have.

The average weekly maximum payment under worker's comp is currently about $450; the average minimum, where one exists, runs about $90 a week. Where there is a permanent total disability, most states pay benefits for an employee's lifetime. The obvious drawback to depending on worker's comp (besides the minimal benefit levels) is that you qualify for benefits only if your injury is work-related. If you think you may be eligible for such compensation, contact your state's Dept. of Labor for details.

A veteran whose disability stems from a service-related illness or injury is eligible to receive benefits. And five states —California, Hawaii, New Jersey, New York, and Rhode Island—have disability funds. These cover illnesses and injuries that aren't work-related, but mostly for a short term. Each state has its own guidelines on how much workers receive in benefits and for how long. In California, for example, the program pays $50 to $336 a week, for up to 52 weeks, depending on a doctor's certification. In New Jersey benefits are paid for no more than 26 weeks, and the maximum paid currently is $339 a week.

The Social Security system also provides long-term disability coverage. The most important thing to know about this coverage is that it is extremely difficult to qualify for.

Generally, Social Security considers you disabled if you are unable to do any kind of work for which you are suited and your disability is expected to last for at least a year or to result in death. Benefits begin six months after you're found to be disabled and range from about $500 to about

$2,000 a month—an amount that a family might have a tough time living on.

An informative pamphlet on Social Security disability (SSA Publication No. 05-10153) is available from any local Social Security office, but financial planners counsel that consumers can't count on this program and must build a safety net around it. In 1995, 61 percent of the people who applied for benefits were turned down. There are attorneys whose entire practice consists of appealing Social Security disability claims that have been axed.

THE HALLMARKS OF A GOOD POLICY

☞ **Look for benefits that replace at least 60 percent of your income.**
Insurers won't cover you for more, since they want you to have an incentive to return to work. Be prepared to prove your income to insurers. Note that many have a cap on the monthly benefit they'll pay. Some group plans won't pay more than $5,000 a month. (There are similar caps on many individually purchased disability policies, too.)

☞ **An employer-paid policy that replaces 60 percent of your income could, after taxes, end up replacing only about 40 percent of your income.**
Can I say this often enough? If your employer offers a long-term disability insurance policy, examine it. If it provides adequate coverage, it's probably the best deal you can get, since, like any group insurance policy, it charges premiums that are discounted from individual policy rates.

But strangely enough, because of a quirk in the tax laws, you're better off paying the entire premium yourself and not having your employer pick up the tab for the insurance. If you have paid the premiums, benefits are tax-free. If the boss pays, benefits are fully taxable—a provision that could cost you plenty and reduces your effective coverage.

👉 **If you receive a good chunk of your annual compensation in commissions or bonuses, check your group policy to see if they're covered.**

Many policies cover only salary. If that's the case with yours, consider buying additional coverage.

👉 **Pay attention to the all-important "definition of disability" in a policy.**

There are three kinds of coverage: own-occupation, any-occupation, and income-replacement. They differ in how they define disability. The definitions go to the pivotal point in disability coverage: when do you qualify for benefits? Most disputes that arise in claiming disability benefits come from confusion about what it takes to be considered disabled.

Own-occupation (own-occ) coverage will pay benefits if you can't work at your specific occupation, be it cardiologist or CPA. Any-occupation (any-occ) means you must be unable to work at any occupation for which your education and training suit you. Income-replacement policies replace the income you can't earn—or whatever portion of it you can't replace.

Own-occ policies are becoming rarer. They are considered the Cadillac of policies, costing as much as 30 percent more than, say, income-replacement policies. That's because they're expensive for companies. A surgeon, for example, who sustained a hand injury and could no longer perform surgery might be perfectly capable of teaching medicine or becoming a hospital administrator. Under an own-occ policy, he or she could take such a job and collect the full salary plus full disability benefits, ending up with more than 100 percent of his or her income before the disability.

Many policies, particularly group disability policies, provide own-occ coverage for, say, the first five years. After that the policy converts to any-occ. This means that if you can apply your skills and education to another gainful occupation, you're expected to do so. That's a perfectly reasonable provision.

You're well served by an income-replacement policy, which is cheaper than an own-occ or any-occ policy. If you're disabled and can't do your job, or a job that pays what your old job did, you're eligible for benefits that will bring you up to your old compensation level.

What you don't want is a policy that says something like this: "disability means total and continuous disability that will prevent the insured from performing any duty pertaining to any business or occupation." That would effectively deny benefits to almost anyone. To be honest, that definition is fairly rare in policies these days, but it is to be avoided at all costs.

☞ **If your savings and resources can support it, a longer waiting period can reduce the price of coverage dramatically.**
There is typically a waiting period before benefits start. During this time, you would depend on sick leave, short-term disability payments, and personal savings and resources. Think of the waiting period as a deductible. Just as an auto-insurance policy with a low deductible is more expensive, so is a disability policy with a very short waiting period. A waiting period of 90 days before you are eligible for benefits is reasonable. If you can manage a longer wait, you'll save even more.

For example, at UNUM Life Insurance Co., if a 40-year-old nonsmoking white-collar worker earning $50,000 in income opted for a waiting period of 90 days, he would pay $644.68 a year for a monthly disability benefit of $2,500 (replacing 60 percent of his salary). If the employee boosted the waiting period to 180 days, the premium would drop to $594.01. Remember, missing the first few months' paychecks might not be catastrophic. You may be able to cover your expenses during that period from your savings. What is ruinous is missing years of income. Even longer waiting periods are possible—a year, for instance. A few companies sell policies with waiting periods of 730 days.

☞ **Look for a benefit period that will cover you until at least age 65.**

What you're really concerned about is how long benefits last. Many group policies provide benefits for only two to five years. If you were critically injured in a car accident and disabled for decades, a two-to-five-year disability policy would delay, but not prevent, financial collapse. You need coverage till you are 65. The presumption is that after that, Social Security will kick in and provide you with an income.

Lifetime benefits, once common, are becoming increasingly rare and expensive, adding perhaps 25 percent to your premium. Lifetime benefits might be worth it if you are in your 20s and haven't had time to qualify for Social Security or pension benefits.

☞ **Make sure the policy allows for residual benefits.**

Without residual benefits, a policy won't pay anything unless you are completely incapable of working. You may be sick enough that you can't work full-time but can manage a reduced schedule. You may also be well enough to take a job but not the demanding one you used to have. Either situation would result in a lower salary than you had predisability. If this happens, residual benefits will pay you part of your salary. Say you're a salesperson who can no longer travel and therefore can earn only half your old salary. Residual benefits would pay you half your full disability payment. Some companies include residual benefits in their policies; others require you to add them as riders.

Beware of "partial benefits," a term often used to describe a feature that pays a set amount of a benefit but only for a short period, often limited to a year.

☞ **Check whether your policy is "noncancelable" or "guaranteed renewable." They sound like they mean the same thing, but they don't.**

Individual disability policies come in two basic flavors: noncancelable and guaranteed-renewable. Noncancelable policies have fixed premiums throughout the life of the contract. When you buy such a policy, you're assured that your premiums will never rise. With guaranteed-renewable policies, the insurer can raise premium rates if it does so for all policies in a certain class. Insurers have to petition state insurance departments for approval to do this, but if they can prove their claims are much higher than expected, they'll get the go-ahead.

Neither type of policy will allow an insurer to drop you if you develop a bad medical history, but there is currently a debate in the industry as to which is better. UNUM Life Insurance Co., which is one of the largest underwriters of disability insurance, is phasing out noncancelable policies and will offer only guaranteed renewable. By doing this, company representatives say, UNUM can limit its losses and reduce premiums for buyers by 10 percent or so. Other insurers (most notably Paul Revere Insurance Group, now part of Provident Life and Accident) have announced that they will continue to sell noncancelable policies to consumers who don't mind paying extra for the assurance of premiums that are fixed for the contract. Provident splits the difference on its main disability policy: it sells a noncancelable income-replacement policy or a guaranteed-renewable own-occ policy.

HOW MUCH DISABILITY SHOULD YOU BUY?

THE INSURANCE COMPANY has a vested interest in making sure you don't have too much disability insurance. The theory is that if you can get paid 100 percent of what you were making predisability, you're not going to have much motivation to go back to work. Insurers like to talk about the "dignity of work" and the psychological need for people to do meaningful work. But just to make sure you have a financial motive to go back to punching the old time clock, most companies will insure you only up to a limit of 60 percent (or sometimes 80 percent) of your current salary.

If you have an investment portfolio or other non-earned income that can cover a large part of your living expenses, or if you and your spouse can manage on one income instead of two, you may want to consider insuring yourself for less than 60 percent of salary. But our recommendation is to buy what you can: unforeseen expenses are just too common.

RUNNING THROUGH WHAT-IF scenarios isn't fun, but it is essential to understanding how much coverage you need and avoiding over- (or under-) insuring yourself. You need to ask yourself what your basic monthly costs are and what your resources are.

Tally up your household's monthly sources of income: salary, interest from any bank or investment accounts, income from any other investments, and your spouse's earnings. You might be able to collect Social Security benefits, but you can't bank on them. If you do qualify, consider it a bonus.

Now add up your monthly expenses, including mortgage and home-ownership costs or rent; food; any debts, such as car loans or credit-card bills; clothing; and other basic insurance costs. (Don't forget utility costs, basic health-care costs, and your educational or entertainment budget.) Subtract the expenses from the income, and you have a rough idea of how much in monthly income you're trying to replace in an emergency.

As we mentioned earlier, insurers will rarely cover you for more than 60 percent of your income. But that may well be enough. If you're disabled, your working expenses will be cut, along with your taxes, and you can scale back your lifestyle a bit. What you want to avoid is losing your home or all your life's savings.

In trying to decide how long a waiting period you could swing before needing benefits, ask your employee-benefits manager what short-term benefits you might qualify for in an emergency, such as sick leave or a state short-term disability fund. Take into consideration the rainy-day savings and investments you could tap for cash.

DISABILITY ADD-ONS DON'T ALWAYS PAY

ANY NUMBER OF OPTIONAL riders are available for disability policies. Like options on a car, many would be nice to have, but they come at a price that might not be worth paying.

Option to increase coverage: This gives you the option to buy more disability coverage without being turned down for health reasons. If you're 55 or older, you're not statistically likely to see a huge percentage increase in your income, so skip it. The option is useful and recommended, however, if you are fairly young: as your income rises you can step up your coverage. Most workers in their 20s and 30s still have substantial income rises ahead of them.

"I have a client who is a partner in a publishing business," says Paul Love, a Bethesda, Maryland, insurance agent. "He suffers from bad migraine headaches that he's been hospitalized for and which have to be regulated by medication. If we tried to get disability for him now, some underwriter at an insurance company would stick holes in his application. But because he had a future-insurability rider, we can buy more insurance periodically without having to qualify medically for coverage." The extra cost for such a rider? According to USAA, a direct-quote insurer (see "Resources," page 224), a 35-year-old male nonsmoker buying a policy providing $3,500 a month in benefits would pay approximately 10 percent more for a rider that allows him to increase his coverage to a maximum of $5,500 a month. (The 10 percent extra charge is for the option of increasing coverage. As you raise coverage, your annual premium would rise proportionately.)

Cost-of-living rider: A cost-of-living (COL) rider increases your monthly benefits after you're disabled. It's a lovely provision but comes at a high price. Tacking on a COL rider can add anywhere from 20 to 40 percent to premiums. If premium dollars aren't a concern, take it. But with inflation currently at fairly low and constant rates, you're better off with an option to increase coverage than with a COL rider. If inflation does heat up, you can increase your insurance.

Social Security rider: This option, also known as the social insurance substitute rider, allows the insurance company to reduce your benefits if you are among the small percentage of people who qualify for Social Security disability benefits. Adding it cuts your premium, saving you money. This makes a lot of sense. After all, you don't really care where your benefits are coming from, as long as you get the sum you need. But take a good look at how much it saves you. Some firms give you a substantial discount in your premium for accepting such a provision: USAA, for example, would cut $127.40 off the premium of the hypothetical policyholder cited above. Other firms may give you a smaller discount.

Waiver-of-premium rider: This provision allows you to stop paying disability premiums if you're disabled, as Marilyn Barnewell was able to. Otherwise, to keep a policy in force—and to keep benefits coming—you have to continue paying. But again, look carefully at what it costs. It may be that with your benefits it's fairly painless to keep paying the premium.

Return-of-premium rider: Consider this a marketing ploy, and stick with straight disability coverage. A skeptic might think insurers have added this rider for the sole purpose of muddying the waters of disability coverage. A return-of-premium rider says that if you don't collect on disability claims, you get some percentage of your premium back. You usually are required to have had the policy in force for a number of years; companies vary on specific conditions. Some will pay even if you've had small disability claims; with others, any disability claims will make you ineligible for a return of premium.

This is an expensive rider, adding as much as 50 percent to the base cost of the coverage. You're overpaying on the premium in hopes of getting some of it returned to you.

THE MAJOR PLAYERS IN DISABILITY

Buying a policy from a company with strong financial ratings is absolutely essential. You want to lock into a policy while you're healthy, and you don't want to have to go shopping for more disability because your insurer goes belly-up. "You don't want your insurance company to die before you do," says Paul Love, a Bethesda, Maryland, insurance agent. "I look for a top rating—in the top three or four rating categories of A.M. Best, Standard & Poor's, Weiss, or Duff & Phelps." The leading companies in disability insurance—which account for more than 50 percent of the market in disability-insurance sales—include the following.

Northwestern Mutual Life Insurance, Milwaukee, Wisconsin (414-271-1444)

Provident Life and Accident Co., Chattanooga, Tennessee (423-755-1011). (Acquired **Paul Revere Insurance Group,** also a large disability seller, in 1996. Provident will continue, for now, to sell policies under both names. Existing Paul Revere policies will continue unchanged.)

UNUM Life Insurance Co. of America, Portland, Maine (207-770-2211)

DISABILITY INSURANCE COMPANIES have had big losses over the past few years, as claims have climbed higher than they expected. How does this affect you?

One of the most dramatic shifts is away from the older, benefit-rich policies. Getting an own-occupation, noncancelable lifetime policy is now prohibitively expensive—if it is even available. Companies are often restricting benefits for mental and emotional disorders, paying perhaps only two or five years of benefits for such claims. And many are limiting monthly benefits to, say, $5,000 or $10,000. That means that even if you earn $500,000 a year and you're willing to pay a lot in disability premiums, you may not be able to replace your income fully. And since claims have been especially high in California and Florida, rates for residents of those states are higher than for those in other areas of the country.

If you're a doctor, my sympathies. (As far as disability-insurance coverage goes, that is. By any other measure, you're still one of society's blessed.) In the past few years, claims by physicians have been so much higher than insurers expected that they're casting a jaundiced eye at your entire profession and taking steps to cut the coverage available to you. Some companies are classifying physicians in a higher-risk—and thus more expensive—category than before. Others have an embargo on the kind of coverage that was previously preferred by physicians (and aggressively marketed to them): own-occ, noncancelable.

Fortunately, in the past five years more-affordable plain-vanilla, no-frills policies, such as income-replacement policies, have been introduced.

☞ **Shop for low-load, or lower-expense, disability insurance.**
Typical insurance-agent commissions on disability policies run 40 to 60 percent of the first-year premium and as high as 25 percent of the next few years' renewal premiums, scal-

ing down to 10 to 15 percent after five years. The good news is that low-load disability policies are becoming more widespread. In 1996, Wholesale Insurance Network (800-808-5810) began selling a Provident disability policy. WIN's chief marketing officer, Dick Weber, estimates that premiums are 20 to 25 percent cheaper through his service than through an agent. USAA (800-531-8000) also sells disability. If you're shopping for a policy, compare the premiums of services like these with the quotes you get from an agent.

☞ **If you're young and on a very tight budget, consider an annual renewable disability income (ARDI) policy.**
This is similar to a term life-insurance policy, where premiums rise as you age and the chances of your becoming disabled increase. Like term life, it makes coverage affordable when you most need it: when you're young. As premiums rise, so will your income and your ability to switch to a level-premium policy. Typically, these policies allow you to convert.

☞ **If you're an individual hunting for coverage, consider hooking up with a group.**
Rates will generally be lower for an alumni group or a professional association. But there's a big caveat here: examine the policy provisions carefully. Some group policies are very restrictive in how long they'll pay benefits, for instance. If you need supplemental disability insurance to shore up the coverage provided by your employer, try buying through the company that provides the group policy. You may get a discount.

☞ **If you're a woman, look for a company that charges unisex rates.**
Women have higher disability rates than men do; however, for the past several years, companies have been pricing policies on a unisex basis. That's now changing, and policy prices for women are going up (although premiums for men don't seem to be falling). Only one state, Montana, requires gender-blind pricing.

☞ **Ask about discounts.**

Some firms give discounts to people who don't smoke. Provident, for instance, charges smokers 20 to 40 percent more for coverage.

IF YOU'VE HAD MEDICAL problems and are trying to get coverage, keep shopping. Some insurers will cover conditions that others won't. Another possibility is to "rider-out" a condition, as agents phrase it. That involves getting coverage for disabilities caused by ailments other than the one specified. If you're a construction worker who has had knee problems, for instance, you may have trouble getting coverage. But you may be able to get a policy that eliminates benefits having to do with your knees. That way, if you have a stroke or heart attack, you'll have disability coverage.

Life
INSURANCE

Where Ratings Reign

N O ONE WANTS to contemplate their own mortality. But every once in a while it is a useful exercise. To judge your life-insurance needs adequately, you need to think about what would happen if you died anytime soon. Only then can you determine whether or not you even need life insurance and, if so, how much of what kind and for how long a term.

What obligations would your death leave behind that an insurance payment could cover? To answer this, ask yourself another simple question: Who is financially dependent on you?

If you have a spouse, children, or elderly parents who depend on you for support, you probably do need life insurance. If you're a child, or if you're single and have some money in the bank, or are married to someone capable of self-support, you probably don't.

Sometimes single people who have no
dependents buy enough insurance to pay off any
debts and burial expenses or to leave a charitable
bequest. Someone I know has a policy on herself
because she has a handicapped brother for whom
she wants to be able to provide. But typically,
single people buy life insurance because they've
been warned that they'll be unable to get it if
their health declines in the near future. Don't
fall for it. The statistical chances of that happening
are slim, unless you're at risk for a fatal disease

like AIDS. In any case, if you don't have to provide for dependents, it may not really matter whether you have life insurance. (Disability insurance for singles is another matter; see "Disability Insurance," page 112.)

Similarly, I've never heard a good reason to insure a child's life, barring the rare cases where he or she supports the family. Better to tuck away the premium money in a college-savings account for the kid.

Should you insure a stay-at-home spouse? Maybe. But only if there's money left in your budget after taking care of your first priority: protecting the family income-stream by adequately insuring the breadwinner. If you have very young children, insuring the homemaker is more important. Full-time day care and household help isn't cheap. It becomes less necessary when there are other family members you can rely on or if your children are teenaged and able to pitch in and help.

HOW MUCH LIFE INSURANCE SHOULD YOU HAVE?

JACK BENNY USED TO TELL this joke: "I don't want to tell you how much insurance I carry with the Prudential, but all I can say is: when I go, they go."

Ideally, you should have enough insurance to allow your family members to continue the lifestyle they were living before your death. But unlike Jack Benny, you don't want too much insurance. There's no sense paying for more than you need. Besides, nobody likes the idea of being worth more dead than alive.

These days, a life-insurance agent who comes to your home will pull out a very impressive-looking laptop and tap in numbers to figure out how much coverage you should get. But you are perfectly capable of making a good estimate yourself using only a pencil and paper, and perhaps a calculator if your addition and subtraction skills are rusty. Here are some do-it-yourself strategies:

Method 1. Use a worksheet like the one on the following page. It won't take long, and because it's specific to your situation, it will provide a more customized picture of your needs than the shortcut method we'll get to in a minute. The worksheet shown is from insurance quote service Wholesale Insurance Network (WIN) and is one of the best I've seen. Keith Maurer, WIN's president, says it was developed with input from financial planners and then refined after tests showed that consumers were confused by or unwilling to complete longer forms.

We've filled in a "John Doe" profile to give you an idea of some typical figures. If you own a business or have assets that are difficult to value, you'll probably need help from a fee-only financial planner. But for most people, this worksheet will work fine.

Method 2. If you're not convinced that your family's security and future happiness are worth taking the 15 minutes required to fill out the worksheet, use the lazy man's and woman's shortcut. Bob Hunter, founder and head of the National Insurance Consumer's Organization, which is now part of the Consumer Federation of America, recommends this rule of thumb: if you have two or more small children, your coverage should equal five to eight times your family income. He points out that many more-complicated ways of calculating your insurance needs require you to estimate what interest rates will be, which is a highly chancy business.

Method 2 has speed to recommend it, but it is short on specifics. If you have a small mortgage and lots of savings, you can lean toward the five-times-salary end of the range. If you have a crippling mortgage, high credit-card debt, and a spouse who will have trouble finding a job, you may need to tilt toward the eight-times-income end.

HOW MUCH INSURANCE SHOULD YOU BUY?

First, how much money do your family members need each year to continue living the way they do now?

			example
Calculate your current living expenses.................. $_____ (including food, clothing, rent or mortgage payments, taxes, utilities, entertainment)	a	60,000
Child care .... $_____ (anticipated cost if one person dies)	b	3,000
Ongoing parent/grandparent care $_____	c	–
TOTAL ANNUAL EXPENSE a+ b + c = $_____	d	63,000
Income of surviving spouse .... $_____	e	25,000
Social Security benefit .... $_____	f	22,000
TOTAL ANNUAL EXPECTED INCOME .... e + f = $_____	g	47,000
Annual expected shortfall Annual expense minus annual expected income d − g =$_____	h	16,000

Second, what are the lump-sum expenses?

Other debts your family will have to pay .... $_____ (automobile, credit-card balances, etc.)	i	10,000
Estimated funeral and administrative expenses .... $_____	j	8,000
Uninsured medical expenses ...... $_____	k	10,000

Children's future
educational needs .... $_____   I _150,000_
Subtotal of
lump-sum expenses   i + j + k + l $_____   m _178,000_

Annual expense shortfall projected
over 10 years .... h x 10 yrs $_____   n _160,000_

TOTAL OF LUMP SUM AND
FUTURE EXPENSES .... m + n $_____   o _338,000_

Third, what sources of income would be available to your
surviving dependents?

Existing life insurance .... $_____   p   _50,000_
Income-producing assets .... $_____   q   _25,000_
(stocks, bonds, rental income, etc.)
Cash and savings accounts .... $_____   r   _10,000_
Social Security benefits .... $_____   s   _255_
(onetime standard benefit)

TOTAL ASSETS .... p + q + r + s = $_____   t   _85,255_

Now subtract

TOTAL ASSETS .... t $_____   _85,255_
from
TOTAL OF LUMP-SUM
AND FUTURE EXPENSES ...... o $_____   _338,000_

TOTAL INSURANCE NEED ... o − t = $_____   _252,745_

Method 3. If you need to be prodded through the process, call the telephone term-quote services listed later in this chapter. Most have representatives who will walk you through the questions on worksheets like the one in Method 1, and you are under no obligation to buy anything.

WHEN YOU'RE FIGURING how much insurance you have to buy based on these calculations, don't forget that part of your needed coverage may already be supplied by the employer-provided life insurance included in

SOCIAL SECURITY'S CONTRIBUTION TO YOUR SAFETY NET

Approximate Monthly Survivors Benefits for Your Family
If You Had Steady Earnings and Die in 1996

YOUR AGE	FAMILY
35	Spouse and 1 child [2]
	Spouse and 2 children [3]
	1 Child only
	Spouse at age 60 [4]
45	Spouse and 1 child [2]
	Spouse and 2 children [3]
	1 Child only
	Spouse at age 60 [4]
55	Spouse and 1 child [2]
	Spouse and 2 children [3]
	1 Child only
	Spouse at age 60 [4]

[1] Earnings equal to or greater than the OASDI wage base from age 22 through 1995

[2] Amounts shown also equal the benefits paid to two children if no parent survives or surviving parent has substantial earnings

many benefits packages. This usually covers a year's
salary. The government also chips in: if you die and
leave behind young children, Social Security will pay a
monthly survivor's benefit to your family. Use the
chart below to help calculate how much of a benefit
your family would reap.

A brief note on how insurance proceeds are taxed.
Generally, the death benefit your insurance pays your
beneficiaries is not taxed. This might not hold true,
however, if you were not the one who actually bought
the policy. If, for example, the purchaser was your

	EARNINGS IN 1995			
$20,000	$30,000	$40,000	$50,000	$61,200 OR MORE[1]
$1,179	$1,580	$1,801	$1,989	$2,150
1,457	1,842	2,101	2,320	2,508
589	790	900	994	1,075
562	753	858	948	1,025
1,179	1,580	1,801	1,975	2,081
1,457	1,842	2,101	2,303	2,427
589	790	900	987	1,040
562	753	858	941	992
1,179	1,579	1,766	1,878	1,946
1,457	1,841	2,060	2,190	2,270
589	789	883	939	973
562	752	842	895	927

[3] Equals the maximum family benefit
[4] Amounts payable in 1996. Spouses turning 60 in the future
would receive higher benefits
Note: The accuracy of these estimates depends on the pattern
of your earnings in prior years

SOURCE: SOCIAL SECURITY ADMINISTRATION

business partner or the partnership or corporation in which you are a partner, shareholder, or officer, some of the death benefit may be taxable.

WHAT TYPE OF POLICY?

NO MATTER HOW YOU CALCULATE it, the dollar amount of insurance you need will no doubt cause your heart to pound and your jaw to drop, particularly if you have a few children and the standard middle-class financial obligations (mortgage, car payments, and the like) and aspirations (college degrees for your children). Don't worry. If you choose your policy carefully, you can probably afford it.

Life insurance is infamous for its confusion factor. Policies come in all flavors, with add-on riders to further complicate matters. But buying life coverage needn't be as confusing as some agents and companies make it.

Part of the confusion stems from what seems to be the infinite variety of policies offered. The different types will be discussed in detail later in the chapter. For now, though, relax—they're all really just variations on two basic themes: term and cash-value life insurance.

Both term and cash-value policies work on the same fundamental premise: you pay the insurance company a premium, and if you die it pays the beneficiaries a death benefit. Beyond that, though, there are important differences.

Term life insurance provides pure protection: If you die while term coverage is in effect, the insurance company pays. If you don't die within the term of coverage, you're happy and the company is happy and your beneficiaries don't get paid anything. The protection provided is "temporary," because the policy covers only a certain term, usually a year. You pay annual premiums that start out relatively low and rise a bit each year, reflecting the increased probability, as you get older, that the insurer will have to pay out.

In contrast, cash-value insurance—including the whole-life, universal, and variable-life varieties—provides a savings and investment plan as well as lifelong protection. Because it provides lifelong coverage, it's often also called "permanent" life, especially by companies and insurance agents who are anxious to portray it in a flattering, Gibraltar-like light.

A cash-value premium has two components: the mortality charge, which pays for the life-insurance portion of the policy, and the reserve, which is invested by the insurance company and builds up value, tax-deferred, that you can tap into, if you wish, or use as collateral for a loan from the company. In the early years, the premium payments are significantly higher for cash-value than for term life insurance—10 times higher for a typical whole-life policy. But cash-value premiums do not rise yearly, as most term premiums do, and may even decrease if the returns from the savings portion of your policy grow sufficiently to cover the mortality charge.

Because of their high premiums, cash-value policies are unwise for many young families. But for those with substantial assets who are making full use of other tax-deferred investment vehicles, cash-value insurance has its uses. For instance, the policies can serve estate-planning purposes.

ANOTHER REASON FOR CONFUSION about life insurance is that it is sold by two kinds of insurance companies, in which policyholders play two kinds of roles: mutual insurers are owned by their policyholders; stockholder insurance companies are owned by their shareholders. As a rule, mutual insurers sell participating, or par, policies, which pay the holders dividends when the insurers' costs have been lower or their revenues higher than anticipated. This isn't quite like getting dividends on stock you might own, since insurance dividends can be considered in part a refund of premiums you overpaid. Most stock companies sell nonparticipating, or nonpar, policies, which never pay dividends. There is crossover, however, with some mutuals marketing a few nonpar, and some stock companies par, policies.

You can take par policies' dividends in cash, or you can use them to pay part of your insurance premiums or to buy more insurance. Dividends can also be "reinvested," added to the cash value of your policy. They're nontaxable, since they're considered a return of excess premiums paid—unless, of course, you get back more than you paid in, in which case the excess is taxable.

Which type of company is better? With term policies, there's not much difference: the dividends have tended to be pretty small, since term premiums are lower. For cash-value policies, it is a bit more complicated. In the past, although mutual companies generally charged higher premiums for cash-value policies, the dividends they paid consumers with participating policies more than offset the difference. But as mutual-fund advertisements always say, past performance is no guarantee of future results.

A more important distinction among insurers involves their financial stability. Don't take out a policy before checking on the company's rating grade.

A GUIDE TO INSURER RATINGS: WHEN A+ IS NOT THE TOP GRADE

THOUGH IT'S NEVER PLEASANT to be a customer of an insurance company that is having financial troubles, it's far worse with certain types of coverage. Consumers shopping for life or disability insurance or health coverage need to be even more vigilant about their insurers' fiscal fitness than buyers of auto and homeowners coverage.

There's a simple reason why you need to worry

about the financial stability of your life-insurance company: you don't want it to die before you do. You're depending on your insurer to be around and have enough assets to pay your beneficiaries. "You want a company you can feel comfortable turning your back on," says Elliot Lipson, an Atlanta-based fee-only financial planner and insurance adviser.

Your company's health is important while you're alive, too. If it fails, you might be forced to buy another policy at a bad time, such as after you've had medical problems. You may decide to dump your insurer (especially with the competitive term-life-insurance rates these days), but you don't want your insurer to dump you. A new policy invariably means a new physical examination, and if you've had serious health problems, it can be difficult and expensive to get coverage.

With a cash-value policy, the stakes are particularly high. Your insurer is holding your money—the cash value that has built up in your policy. You stand to lose much of that if the company runs into financial trouble.

When an insurer stumbles, regulators step in. Sometimes they reorganize the company or have it taken over by a stronger insurer. In the meantime they freeze its assets, though they generally allow death benefits to be paid if a policyholder dies while a company is being reorganized. Most states have guaranty laws that protect life-insurance policyholders, but there are caps and limits on what they'll pay on the cash value built up in a policy. And sometimes policyholders get far less in the way of a settlement than they expected—something on the order of 70 cents on the dollar. It's not a situation that you want to find yourself in.

THE BEST WAY TO TELL whether an insurance company is solid and solvent is to look at its ratings from the independent rating agencies: Weiss Ratings, A.M. Best, Duff & Phelps, Moody's Investors Service, and

AGENCIES AND THEIR RATINGS

SECURE RATINGS:

A.M.BEST	DUFF & PHELPS	MOODY'S	STANDARD & POOR'S	WEISS
A++, A+	AAA	Aaa	AAA	A+ to A-
A, A-	AA+ to AA-	Aa1 to Aa3	AA+ to AA-	B+ to B-
B++, B+	A+ to A-	A1 to A3	A+ to A-	C+ to C-
B, B-	BBB+ to BBB-	Baa1 to Baa3	BBB+ to BBB-	

VULNERABLE RATINGS:

A.M.BEST	DUFF & PHELPS	MOODY'S	STANDARD & POOR'S	WEISS
C++, C+	BB+ to BB-	Ba1 to Ba3	BB+ to BB-	D+ to D-
C, C-	B+ to B-	B1 to B3	B+ to B-	
D	CCC+ to CCC-	Caa, Ca, C	CCC	E+ to E-
E, F	DD		R	F

SOURCE: GAO, COS.

Standard & Poor's Corp. The agencies study a company's financial reports and in some cases assess its management to come up with a grade that describes how strong its financial house is.

Be careful using these ratings. The same grade coming from different agencies may mean different things: A+, for instance, is Weiss's highest rating, Best's second-highest, but only fifth-highest on the Duff & Phelps and Standard & Poor's lists. And not all insurance companies are rated. In some cases, the absence of a rating merely means the insurer hasn't paid the fee many of the agencies charge to produce one. Weiss, however, doesn't charge insurers a fee and, according to a 1994 report by the General Accounting Office, rates most insurers. All agencies, moreover, cover the companies that together provide at least 50 percent of the insurance in this country.

Even a high grade doesn't ensure lasting stability. Companies can stumble quickly and without much warning. Executive Life, Mutual Benefit, and Con-

federation Life Insurance all ran into trouble not
long after receiving secure ratings from agencies.
Your best course of action is to buy from an insurer
that is given high marks by at least three of the raters.
A.M. Best is the best known of the rating agencies,
but Weiss is widely considered to be the toughest
grader of the group.

Your insurance agent should notify you when your
insurer is downgraded. But if you have cash value
accumulating in a policy, you should check the ratings
periodically yourself and keep a sharp eye out for
reports of ratings drops.

Most public libraries have insurer-rating guides available for readers to check. The agencies will also provide information over the telephone, at these numbers:

◆ **A.M. Best:** BestLine is 800-424-BEST or 900-555-
BEST. The cost is $4.95 per rating.
◆ **Duff & Phelps:** The Consumer Hotline for ratings
is 312-368-3198. Ratings are free.
◆ **Moody's:** Consumers can call 212-553-0377 for up
to three free rankings per phone call.
◆ **Standard & Poor's:** The Ratings Desk at 212-208-
1527 will provide free information to consumers.
◆ **Weiss Ratings:** Consumers can get Weiss rankings
for $15 each by calling 800-289-9222.

GETTING INSURED

ONCE YOU'VE DECIDED you need life insurance and
have an idea of how much and which of the two basic
types best serves your needs, it's time to do some shopping. One approach is to call a local life-insurance
agent. An insurance sales agent either sells for one
company or is an independent contractor who has
established relationships with a group of companies
that pay commissions for each policy sold.

The commissions are smaller for term policies.
That's why agents so often try to nudge customers into
cash-value insurance. Consider that an agent selling a

whole-life policy for $100,000 might garner a commission equal to the entire first year's premium, more than $1,000. Some companies pay more than 100 percent of the first year's premium to agents, as a sort of loss-leader to get business.

And there are commissions on premiums paid after the first year. "In a whole-life policy, the commission in years two to four might be 5 to 10 percent of the premium," says Glenn Daily, a fee-only insurance consultant and the author of *The Individual Investor's Guide to Low-Load Insurance Products*. "After that they go down to about 5 percent, and after the 10th year, they're 3 percent or less."

Even in a state like New York, where commissions are limited to 55 percent of the first year's premium, the agent in the example above would take in $500. The commission on a similar term policy might be 35 to 55 percent of the first year's premium of $150, or $52.50 to $82.50, with subsequent renewal commissions of perhaps 3 to 5 percent, or none at all.

So when you sit down at the kitchen table with an insurance agent, steel yourself for what may be a hard sell. And keep in mind that there are other ways to shop for insurance:

◆ Ask your employee-benefits office about buying additional insurance through any term-life policy your employer provides. It's often a good deal.

◆ Check out the rates on term-life insurance offered by other groups, such as professional and alumni associations. Some are bargains; others aren't.

◆ Look into savings-bank life insurance. In Connecticut, Massachusetts, and New York, savings banks sell life-insurance policies that traditionally have been good deals. If you live in one of those states, call a local savings bank and ask about life policies, or in New York call 1-800-GET-SBLI for information.

◆ Do your own research. For term-life insurance, you can get quotes and other information from one of the quote services (for more information, see page 157). Make a quick call, too, to USAA (800-531-8000) and Ameritas (800-552-3553). These are insurance companies that sell their own term and cash-value policies directly, without any middleman or commission, often at attractive premium savings.

"When I shop for clients, the first call I always make is to USAA," says Janet Briaud, the past president of a fee-only financial planners group. "If anyone can beat them, fine, but usually they're at or near the bottom."

☞ **Ask for each policy's net-payment index number.**
The interest-adjusted net-payment cost index is designed to help you compare costs. In calculations that only an actuary could love, it takes into account the premiums you pay and when you pay them: paying more up front costs you more, because a dollar in hand is worth more to you than one you'll earn down the road. The net-payment number, which will be something like $1.79, tells you the current cost of each $1,000 of insurance in the policy. Please note that this index is suitable only for comparing term policies.

☞ **Get *Consumer Reports* magazine's ratings by writing to CU/Reprints, 101 Truman Avenue, Yonkers, NY 10703-1057 (914-378-2000).**
Consumer Reports periodically does a comprehensive review and rating of term, whole-life, and universal-life insurance policies. As of this writing, the most recent review was published in a series that ran in July, August, and September 1993. Check your local library, or write to *Consumer Reports* at the above address for information on the price of reprints.

IF YOU'RE IN THE MARKET for cash-value insurance, with its higher commissions, the direct sell of USAA and Ameritas is particularly attractive. By reducing commissions you typically allow cash value to build up faster in the policy. Other firms, such as Wholesale

Insurance Network (800-808-5810), sell low-load cash-value policies—written by other companies but carrying low commissions. Low-load cash-value commissions range from 0 to 10 percent of a first year's premium, 1 to 3 percent of later years'. Fee-only advisers can also hunt down low-load cash-value policies.

These services can save you just as much money as discount brokers and no-load mutual funds save equity investors. In fact, discount brokerage firm Charles Schwab & Co. recently began selling no-load life insurance policies. For information and premium quotes, call 1-800-542-LIFE.

You can also save money by hiring an adviser to help you with your insurance buying for a straight hourly fee and asking for a full or partial rebate on the commission. He or she might be willing to comply, to get your business. This approach has serious drawbacks, though. Rebates are illegal in every state except California and Florida, which may be more of a testament to the strength of the insurance agents' lobbyists than to the inherent drawbacks of rebating. Moreover, if you manage to get a rebate by buying a policy in one of those states, the money is taxable and it still doesn't go toward increasing your cash value.

When you buy a life-insurance policy, you will usually be required to take some sort of a physical exam and provide a brief medical history. An insurer will want to know if you smoke, if your parents or siblings died before age 60 (and what they died from), your height and weight, and the details of any medications and medical treatment you've received lately. It will take blood, do a cholesterol check, and in states where it's not prohibited, do an AIDS test. The insurance company also wants to know what you do for a living. Test pilots pay higher premiums than accountants. If you're applying for a large amount of life insurance, the company may request more extensive information. If you want to buy $2 million of coverage

or more, you'll probably have to take a treadmill stress
test. At that level of death benefits, the insurance company wants to know the intricacies of your arteries.

The insurer will use this information to decide what
kind of a risk you are and how much to charge you.
Preferred or "select" risks are generally healthy and so
qualify for the lowest prices. A standard risk is less
than ideal, and a substandard risk is someone who has
problems.

Don't even think of shading the truth on your
insurance application. The omniscient medical-
reporting bureaus probably have files on you (for
more information on medical-reporting firms, see
page 96). What's more important, if you die and the
insurance company finds out you've lied on your
application, it may be able to cancel the policy. The
company generally has two to three years within which
to fight a claim. Even after this period has passed, it
can reduce the death benefits paid to your family to
reflect what your true health status was. (Note: if you
commit suicide within the first two years your policy
is in effect, the insurer will generally not pay your beneficiaries the full death benefit but merely return to
them the premiums you paid.)

Once you sign on the dotted line, you own the policy. That generally means that you are the person who
is insured and paying the premiums. As owner you are
also the one that can tap into the cash value of a cash-
value policy for a loan or withdrawal. And you get to
name the beneficiaries on the policy.

☞ **If you have morning-after regrets about buying
your life-insurance policy, remember that most companies
give you a 10-day free-look period during which you can
change your mind and get a refund.**
Once a policy is in effect, the insurer can't cancel it if you
become ill. Unless you fail to pay the premium, the policy
can't lapse. And if you miss a payment, there is usually a

grace period of about a month during which the insurance remains in effect. After that, if you still haven't paid the balance due, the policy lapses, but you can generally reinstate it for a period of time under certain conditions: you must pay the back premiums, and you may have to prove your health status anew.

👉 **You can change beneficiaries while your policy is in effect; when, how often, and how you go about doing that varies with your insurer.**

Usually, you'd name your children or current spouse as beneficiary. But that doesn't always work. Sometimes divorce settlements dictate that an ex-spouse be named the beneficiary of a life-insurance policy to compensate for the child support and alimony benefits that would cease if the insured died.

👉 **Never make out a premium check to anyone but the insurance company.**

Agents have been known to buy, perhaps accidentally, different policies for their customers than the ones they discussed. In rare cases they have absconded with premiums. "If an individual writing a check makes it payable to the agent, not the insurance company, the individual is at the mercy of the agent," says Barry Schweig, an insurance professor at Creighton University.

THE CASE FOR TERM LIFE INSURANCE

MOST PEOPLE WHO NEED life insurance need term policies. Dollar for dollar, pound for pound, they offer the most coverage for the cheapest price. And in recent years price wars among the leading insurers have made them even cheaper.

A term policy is perfect for young families, whose life-insurance needs are greatest and budgets tightest. The premium on a whole-life policy offering $250,000 or $300,000 in coverage for someone in his mid-30s can be $2,000 or $3,000. The same amount of coverage on a term-life basis costs more like $200 to $300.

Term life has other features to recommend it: it's simple, easy to understand, and lends itself to comparison shopping. It is not an investment; it simply pays your beneficiary a sum of money if you die while the policy is in effect. With level-premium term (see below), you can choose your insurance term to coincide with your period of greatest insurance need. Listen to Robert Hunter: "I'm 59, and the youngest of my six children is just about to enter college. I just locked in term-life rates for the next five years by calling Ameritas. After the five years is up, I'm done with life insurance. I don't need it anymore."

You might torch your term policy about the same time you burn your paid-up mortgage, when the assets you've spent 20 years accumulating are your cushion. "Life insurance protects you against premature death, not too-old death," says Hunter. "Too-late death is when you have to worry about pensions. Life insurance is not something you really want to collect on."

There are two basic types of term policies: annual-renewable term and level-premium term. Annual-renewable term, or ART, is truly the plain-vanilla variety of life insurance. You buy the policy, and the company has to renew if you want it to, but with a premium that rises each year.

☞ **When you're shopping for an ART policy, ask to see the premiums for every year of the term you've selected.** Some companies have very low first-year rates that they raise substantially in the second or third year. Others drop their rates in certain benchmark years—years 1, 5, 10, and 15, for instance—but have price jumps in the other years, which customers are less likely to examine.

A LEVEL-PREMIUM TERM policy locks in its premium at a constant rate for a specified period, typically 5, 10,

15, or 20 years. The rate is higher than the one you'd pay on an annual-renewable policy in the early years but lower than the one you'd probably pay later on. This feature appeals to people who have a definite time during which they want to guarantee coverage. A couple whose youngest child will be out of college in seven years, for example, may go for a 10-year level-premium policy.

👉 Ask what happens when the level period is up.
When a level-premium period is up, some policies specify that your coverage converts to annual-renewable term, while others allow you to renew at a level premium for another 5 or 10 years, after taking a physical. Still others don't allow renewal on any basis. Make sure you're guaranteed access to some sort of policy regardless of your health.

👉 Check that the premium is truly level.
Instead of offering a constant rate, some companies merely guarantee that you will get the preferred rate—the one paid by its healthiest group of policyholders—for each year. If rates on the whole group rise, so do your bills. Read the small print.

👉 Go for "convertible term" insurance.
Often this provision is incorporated into the policy; in some instances, it's available as a rider. It allows you to convert your policy from term to whole life. It's well worth having. If you decide at some point that you want cash-value insurance, this allows you to change your policy without taking another health exam.

OTHER TYPES OF TERM INSURANCE exist, but they make up a small slice of the pie. Decreasing term has lower premiums to begin with and a death benefit that decreases over the years. In theory this makes some sense: you have the most protection at the beginning and the least at the end, when your need may well be smaller. But in practice there is much more competition in annual-renewable and level-premium term, so the prices are better there. Also, a decreasing-term policy locks you into reducing your coverage; better to have the flexibility of annual-renewable if you think you will want to cut your insurance coverage.

Mortgage life insurance pays off your mortgage if you die. The trouble is, if you have a low-cost mortgage and interest rates rise, your surviving spouse might do better to keep the loan and invest the insurance proceeds elsewhere. Sometimes mortgage life is required by the mortgage lender, but if not, I'd skip it. The same holds true for credit life insurance, which pays off your debts if you die. The only advantage of credit life is that it generally doesn't require a medical exam.

☞ **Beware the "You can not be turned down for any reason" sales hook.**
"Guaranteed-issue insurance" is a fancy name for the kind of insurance you see certain celebrities endorsing on television. Don't get skewered by one of these pitches. Not only is this insurance extremely expensive per dollar of benefit, but there's a catch: if you die within the early years of taking out the policy, your beneficiary collects only a small percentage of the death benefit, plus the premiums you paid. These policies exploit the elderly and the desperately ill, both of whom are the least likely to collect on them.

VARIOUS RIDERS MAY ALSO be attached to standard term policies in return for a higher premium. Some are worthwhile; others most definitely aren't.

A waiver-of-premium rider guarantees that if you become disabled, you can stop paying premiums and your life insurance will stay in force. Don't bother. You're better off buying enough disability insurance (see "Disability Insurance," page 112) to cover all your bills if you can't work.

Unless you think you're Barbara Stanwyck in *Double Indemnity,* you can also forget about the accidental-death rider, which doubles the policy payout in case the policyholder dies in an accident. If your heirs and survivors need the extra money, they need it no matter how you die, so just increase your coverage.

Guaranteed future insurability allows you to buy more life insurance at certain specified times—such as on your 30th or 35th birthday—without having a medical exam. If you're over 40, this rider may not be offered to you. It is a useful add-on, since you may need additional life-insurance coverage as the size of your family or financial obligations grow.

THE PAST FEW YEARS have presented another good reason to buy term life insurance: continuing price wars that, as of this writing, had made premiums cheaper than ever before. "I don't know if we've hit bottom yet," says Hunter, "but nobody thinks term rates are going up anytime soon."

Milton Brown, founder and president of Insurance Information, Inc., an insurance quote service that surveys some 600 companies, has tracked the cheapest prices over the past few years for a 20-year, $250,000 level-premium insurance policy on a 35-year-old woman. Those prices, listed below, saw dramatic drops. (All the companies were rated financially secure.)

1991	$447.50
1992	$402.50
1993	$390.00
1994	$347.00
1995	$295.00

"The key to term is shop, shop, shop," says Brown. "Each year it was a different company that was offering one of the lowest rates."

In recent years, several term-life-insurance quote services have set up shop, enabling you to get a quick—and free—idea of the policies and premiums available to you just by dialing an 800 number. Service representatives will ask you how much insurance you're interested in. If you don't have a clue, they will usually walk you through some basic calculations to figure it out. They'll also ask your age and gender and basic health questions. It's important that you answer accurately, because otherwise you could end up getting quotes on policies that you can't qualify for.

The reps then run your information through their computer databases and send you a list of the cheapest policies they could find for you. This typically arrives in the mail within three to five days, but if you're in a hurry, the services are usually willing to fax it to you instead. Along with between 3 and 40 quotes, you get information on the companies, including the all-important financial ratings and, if you ask for it, the interest-adjusted net-payment index.

If you're interested in one of the policies, you can buy it through the quote service, which makes money on commissions, as a regular agent would. Or you can shop elsewhere. The services promise never to call you again, although most send a follow-up letter asking if you received the information they sent and giving you a telephone number to call if you have questions.

It's important to remember that, like any independent life-insurance agency, a quote service has an established relationship with a group of companies. Some deal with perhaps a dozen or 20; others cast a wider net. So you should call a couple of services in your shopping excursion. Below is a sampling of quote services; there are many others.

◆ **InsuranceQuote Services:** 800-972-1104
◆ **Quotesmith:** 800-431-1147
◆ **SelectQuote:** 800-343-1985
◆ **TermQuote:** 800-444-8376

◆ **Wholesale Insurance Network (WIN):**
800-808-5810

Brown's service, Insurance Information, Inc. (800-472-5800), is somewhat different. It is not a sales rep and charges you $50 to scan the 600 companies in its universe. Brown guarantees to find you a cheaper term policy than you have now or he'll give back the $50.

ABOUT CASH VALUE

WHOLE LIFE, UNIVERSAL life, and variable life—they are all variations on the same theme: insurance for which you pay a premium, of which part pays for the death benefit and part accrues on a tax-deferred basis inside your policy. In effect, you're paying more than you would on a term policy in the early years so you can pay less later.

One point of clarification: if you die your beneficiaries receive the stated death benefit, not the death benefit plus the cash value in the policy. If you cancel a policy, though, you keep the cash value, minus certain surrender charges. The major types of cash-value policies are summarized on page 160.

☞ **Don't buy a cash-value policy unless you're sure you can really afford the high premiums year after year.**
Because of the large commissions and administrative charges, most policies don't begin to accumulate much of a cash value until after the first five or seven years. That's too late for a lot of customers: some 25 percent of people drop out in the first two years, and approximately half are gone by the seventh year. The reason? They simply can't keep up the premium payments.

"I think the reason a lot of people drop their policy is that they bought it to get the agent out of the house," says the Consumer Federation's Hunter. "People realize they made a mistake and that it's too much money. It's a hard way to learn."

👉 **Make sure that you see an in-force ledger for your policy once a year.**
This will tell you the exact returns on your cash-value investment. Ask your agent, if you use one, or call the insurance company directly and request it.

WHO SHOULD CONSIDER CASH-VALUE INSURANCE?

CASH-VALUE INSURANCE is often marketed to people in their 20s and 30s as a form of forced savings. That's the wrong reason to buy it. If you honestly think you can't discipline yourself to save, there are cheaper ways to force yourself than by paying cash-value commissions and fees. Buy term insurance, and arrange to have the amount you save on premiums automatically taken out of your paycheck or bank account and invested in a mutual fund.

The main reason to buy a cash-value policy is if you're going to need insurance in your old age, when term premiums are higher. For example, if you're older than 50 and are going to be needing life insurance for a long period, take a look at plain whole-life insurance. At that age the advantages of whole life become more appealing, since term premiums start to rise dramatically.

Two other categories of consumers who might do well to consider a cash-value policy: (a) those who have made full use of other tax-advantaged investment plans, such as retirement plans, and have some life insurance needs and (b) those who have estate-planning concerns—a life-insurance policy can be used to pay estate taxes or buy out a partner's share in a business, for example.

Two variations tailor cash-value policies to tax- and estate-planning purposes. Single-premium life insurance can serve as a tax-deferred investment play and a way to pass down money to your heirs, since death benefits are free of federal income tax. It stands up

MAJOR TYPES OF CASH-VALUE INSURANCE

Whole life, also known as straight life or ordinary life, is the granddaddy of life-insurance policies. It has:

◆ A death benefit.

◆ Premiums that generally stay the same over the life of the policy.

◆ In a traditional whole life policy, cash value that accumulates at a fixed rate. The insurer determines how the money is invested but usually guarantees a minimum return, perhaps 4 percent.

◆ Lifelong coverage, to age 99. After that the policy terminates, and the insured gets a big 100th-birthday check from the insurance company.

◆ In some whole-life policies, the returns paid fluctuate instead of being fixed, although there are usually guaranteed minimum cash values. The rate may be tied to some index or security, or it can be changed at the discretion of the insurance company.

Universal life was popularized in the 1980s in response to consumers' complaints about the low interest rates that were being paid on whole-life cash reserves. Universal life is characterized by:

◆ An adjustable death benefit. You can choose a higher death benefit and lower cash values, or opt for the reverse, and you can change the benefit after the policy is in effect. Increasing it usually requires that you have a medical exam.

◆ Flexible insurance premiums. Within certain specified minimum and maximum limits, you can set your own premium payments. Skipping a payment has important consequences, though: if the investment return and cash reserves on your policy don't cover the mortality charges, you may have to pay larger premiums or let the policy lapse.

◆ Higher administrative costs and fees than for whole life.
◆ A cash value whose return depends on the insurance company's performance and its return on its investment portfolio. There is usually a guaranteed minimum, and the return that you're earning on your reserves is disclosed to you in your statements, unlike in some whole-life policies, where consumers have no idea what specific return rate they're getting.
◆ Lifelong coverage.

Variable life policies further complicate your options. They are characterized by:
◆ A death benefit and a cash value that fluctuate with the returns on a portfolio of investments. Your insurance premium goes not only to paying for the death benefit, but also into investments you choose, such as stock, bond, or money-market funds. Some policies guarantee that the death benefit won't fall below a minimum level.
◆ Flexibility in premium payments. A whole-life variable policy requires you to pay a specified yearly premium; a universal-variable policy lets you alter your premium.
◆ As with universal, higher fees and administrative costs. If the investment you choose (such as a stock mutual fund) doesn't do well, you may have to boost your premium payments to keep your insurance in effect. You can also watch the cash value of your policy rise or drop. These risks are underscored by the fact that variable life policies are considered securities contracts, sold only by agents registered with the National Association of Securities Dealers and are registered with the Securities and Exchange Commission.
◆ Lifelong coverage.

less well as a way to provide for your dependents should you die prematurely. That's because, as pure insurance, it's expensive. You pay one lump-sum premium—maybe $5,000, maybe $50,000—and you're the proud owner of a cash-value life-insurance policy. You pay no more premiums. You earn a return on the cash in your policy that is effectively tax-deferred, and you can borrow against it.

Second-to-die insurance, also called survivorship or joint life insurance, is used mainly by wealthy consumers who are concerned about the taxes that will come due on an estate. The policy covers two people but pays a benefit only on the second death. In a typical scenario, a husband and wife purchase second-to-die insurance so that their estimated estate taxes can be paid without requiring the sale of a business or other sizable assets that they wish to pass on to their children.

☞ **Don't buy second-to-die insurance without speaking with an accountant and attorney who are experienced in estate planning, as well as a fee-only insurance adviser (see "Fee-Only Advisers," page 167) or planner.**
Using such a strategy involves significant tax and legal complications that you can't afford to ignore; for instance, in many cases a second-to-die policy should be in an irrevocable trust to avoid tax problems.

TAKING MONEY OUT OF A CASH-VALUE POLICY

AS YOUR CASH-VALUE BALANCE grows in a whole-life, universal, or other cash-value policy, you might find you need to tap those funds. In fact, the ability to borrow on the cash value of your policy is one of the oft-touted advantages of this kind of life insurance. Once you've built up some cash value in your policy, you can borrow from the insurance company using your balance as collateral. Typically, the loan can be for up to 90 percent of the value of your policy and does not entail the approval process you'd have to go through with other lenders. Loans aren't an option, of course, in the first few years, when there's generally no cash balance to speak of. But later on it can be a way to access your accumulated cash.

👉 **If you die with the loan unpaid, your family may not get the level of protection you planned for them to receive; the outstanding balance and the interest are subtracted from the death benefits.**
Say, for example, you take a $20,000 loan on a $100,000 policy and die before it's repaid. Your family would receive $80,000, rather than the full $100,000 death benefit (not counting any interest payments also due).

THE INTEREST RATES ON POLICY loans tend to be fairly reasonable, anywhere from 5 to 8 percent, depending on how old the policy is. The rate on newer policies is 8 percent or a floating rate tied to an index. Years ago, interest rates on policy loans were so low that policyholders became arbitrageurs, borrowing from their insurers at 4 percent and investing the money at, say, 12 percent. That has changed.

The interest you pay is only part of your loan's cost, however. While it is outstanding, there are also ramifications for your cash value. When you take out a loan, the insurer takes a sum equal to your loan for collateral and sets it aside. That money earns a lower rate of return while the rest of your money, the unencumbered balance, earns the normal rate. So if you're figuring your borrowing costs, don't forget to factor in the amount of interest you'll forgo on the borrowed portion.

Once upon a time, you could deduct the interest on insurance-policy loans on your taxes, but that's not the case anymore. Interest expenses generally aren't deductible except in specific circumstances: if the borrowed funds were used to buy securities, for instance, the interest could be deductible as investment interest.

ANOTHER WAY TO GET ACCESS to your cash value is to cancel the policy and get your money back. Of course, this leaves your family without life-insurance coverage. There may also be a surrender charge, which is a sort of back-end load, when you cancel your policy. And you should consider the tax consequences: if you cancel a cash-value policy and get money back, it may be taxable to the extent that it exceeds the total amount of premiums you paid over the years.

Some policies allow partial withdrawals of money. But those withdrawals, too, can trigger tax implications, depending on considerations such as how long you've held the policy. If you're thinking of making a partial withdrawal, it's best to consult the insurance company and your accountant.

Taking money out of a single-premium policy is complex. The tax code treats such policies sold after 1988 differently from those sold before. (The post–1988 policies are also referred to as "modified endowment contracts.") With a single-premium policy bought before 1988 and not substantially modified since then, you can take out loans against your cash value without incurring any tax liability. With a post–1988 policy, you pay a 10 percent penalty on loans and withdrawals made before age 59½; policyholders of any age also owe federal income tax on withdrawals, and on loans if they are for more than the premiums paid in. If you do decide to take money out of one of these policies, consult an accountant or adviser; it's possible to structure a withdrawal to avoid the penalty. The bottom line: single-premium policies are best for consumers who are older than 59½ and in a high tax bracket.

MAKING SENSE OF LIFE-
INSURANCE "ILLUSTRATIONS"

WHEN AN AGENT IS TRYING to sell you a cash-value policy, the moment will come when he or she unveils the sales illustration, a document that is several pages long and consists of endless columns of numbers. These include the annual premium, the death benefit, and the policy's projected and guaranteed cash values, all calculated for your age and gender.

The illustration is impressive. But remember that it's a sales tool and the figures on it are easily manipulated.

Be particularly wary of those alluring projected cash values. The temptation is to look up what your policy will be worth in 30 years and daydream about having access to those assets. But the figures can be so distorted that there's really no sense in even looking at them. With all cash-value policies, look for the guaranteed minimum return.

The illustration usually doesn't explicitly disclose the interest rate used to figure how the cash in your policy is going to pile up. But it may be unrealistically high. In 1993, when *Consumer Reports* magazine ran a comprehensive series on life insurance, it discovered that the interest rate one major company used in its cash-value projections was from 1980, more than 10 years earlier, when rates were at all-time highs.

Companies can also tinker with mortality rates and assumptions about expenses. They often play games with the dividends paid on participating policies as well. It's important to realize that the dividends are not guaranteed, and if they're cut the cash values on policies are going to grow more slowly.

Projecting cash values at all is controversial. When mutual funds advertise, they are permitted only to cite historical returns, not to make guesses about what future performance will be. Many actuaries believe that policy returns are going to drop in the future as insurers, who are under pressure from regulators and rating agencies, replace high-yielding, riskier securities with lower-yielding, safer ones.

So run a line through any projected cash values, and just look at the guaranteed or cash-surrender values.

The vanishing premium is another marketing ploy you may encounter. I distinctly remember a life-insurance pitch I got in 1986. The agent pointed to the computer-generated chart showing the premiums, death benefit, and cash value on a particular policy. The column listing the premium due was blank after the seventh year. "After that, your policy is paid up," he said. "You're covered by life insurance for the rest of your life, and it doesn't cost you anything."

Well . . . not quite. In theory, vanishing premiums work like this: once you build up a large cash value on your policy, your investment throws off enough money to pay the premium; the policy stays in force without additional payments from you.

When interest rates were high this was a workable premise. But rates have tumbled in recent years, and consumers have gotten unpleasant news from their insurers. If returns fall enough, the companies ask for more money to keep the insurance in place. You may have to make years of additional payments before your policy builds up to the point where you don't need to pay premiums. Otherwise, the policy lapses, or the amount is taken out of cash value. So it's best to view vanishing-premium projections with an extremely skeptical eye.

TWISTING IN THE WIND?

IN THE TRADE, IT'S KNOWN as churning or twisting. That's when an insurance agent convinces a client to drop his or her perfectly good cash-value insurance and buy a new policy. It's always a good deal for the agent, who earns that hefty first-year premium commission. (Be particularly suspicious if your agent

HOW TO FIND FEE-ONLY ADVISERS

Buying a cash-value insurance policy involves dealing with layers of complexity, particularly when there are tax or estate-planning considerations. "Life insurance is extraordinarily complicated, and life-insurance consumers are almost always in the position of having it sold to them rather than rationally reaching out and buying it," says Peter Katt, a West Bloomfield, Michigan, fee-only insurance adviser.

You may feel uncomfortable dealing with an ordinary insurance agent, since his or her recommendations could be influenced by the size of the commission on certain products. In contrast, advisers like Katt work for hourly consulting fees the way an accountant or an attorney would. Katt, who is the author of *The Life Insurance Fiasco: How to Avoid It*, charges $195 an hour; others may have different rates.

To find an adviser, you can consult the Life Insurance Advisers Association (800-521-4578), which was founded by Katt. Another source is Fee for Service (800-874-5662), which can also refer you to fee-only financial planners. If you contact planners in your area, ask specifically about their insurance training and expertise. Credentials such as CLU (chartered life underwriter) indicate that they've had some advanced training in insurance.

shows up with a proposal to flip you into a new policy about five years after selling you your current one, when his or her trailing commissions may have begun to drop off.) But it doesn't always work out so well for the customer.

Switching from one term-life policy to another is no big deal. In fact, with rates dropping, changing to a cheaper policy is probably a good idea for healthy people. Dropping an existing cash-value policy to buy term insurance is another story. Even though term is usually a better initial choice for most consumers, if you have held a cash-value policy for more than a few years, you probably should hold on to it. At that point, you've gotten past the early, expensive years, when commissions and fees eat up most of your cash value, and are finally beginning to accumulate a cash balance. Bailing out, moreover, can involve substantial surrender charges and complex tax considerations.

"I used to say that 90 percent of the time, it doesn't make sense [to switch policies]," says Glenn Daily. "But recently I've seen some crummy policies where the company is providing poor value to the policy owners. It can be worth it, particularly if you're switching to a low-load policy. But I'd still say that most of the time it doesn't make sense."

That's not to say there are no legitimate reasons to trade in a cash-value policy. If you are getting exceptionally bad returns, for instance, or the insurer is facing financial difficulties, it may be better to cut your losses. Ditto if you're switching policies for tax or estate-planning purposes. But buyer beware applies in a big way.

In the past few years, agents for such well-known companies as Prudential and Metropolitan Life have been widely accused of systematically churning customers. A.L. Williams, a term-life insurer now part of Primerica, developed a reputation in the 1980s of getting new customers to drop existing cash-value policies inappropriately to buy its term policies.

How do you protect yourself? Trying to evaluate an agent's proposal to switch is almost impossible, since the sales illustrations for the new policy and the old one may be based on drastically different statistical assumptions. Take careful note of the first-year cash value of the proposed policy, and compare it with the current cash value of your existing policy. Any decrease should be questioned. If you're contacted by a new agent with an attractive-sounding proposal, call your old agent to see if he or she can rebut the arguments.

If I were thinking of switching policies, the first thing I would do is use a service offered by the Consumer Federation of America. Actuaries in the federation's insurance department will compare a proposed policy with your existing one, and give you an unbiased opinion on whether you should switch. The price: $40 for the first illustration and $30 for the second. The service is well worth the money. Contact the CFA at 202-387-6121 for information. Another smart step to take if you're thinking of replacing a policy is to call the American Society of Chartered Life Underwriters & Chartered Financial Consultants (800-392-6900). The group puts out a worksheet that can help you evaluate a prospective switch. "It will discourage agents who are simply doing this for their new commission," says Daily. "It outlines the pros and cons, mentions the new contestability period, the suicide provisions, and any riders, and shows the difference in illustrated values. It takes maybe an hour to fill out, but professional agents won't mind."

☛ **Don't switch just because you've suddenly realized your cash-value policy is too small.**
If you feel drastically underinsured with a policy worth perhaps $50,000, buy additional coverage—through term insurance. And keep the smaller cash-value policy.

☛ **If you do decide that you're going to dump your cash-value policy, don't cancel until you've secured the term or other coverage you're going to get.**

LIVING BENEFITS ON YOUR INSURANCE POLICY

A LIVING-BENEFITS OPTION allows terminally ill people to claim part of the death benefits of a cash-value life-insurance policy before they die. With this money, victims of AIDS, cancer, and other diseases can pay for medical care and other bills and live out their days in comfort and security.

This option—sometimes called accelerated benefits and very like viatical arrangements offered by outside insurers—is included in some policies and may be bought as a rider to others. It generally entitles you to draw on 80 to 90 percent of your policy's face value. If your policy doesn't include living-benefit provisions or riders, you can turn to a viatical settlement company, which will pay you 50 to 80 percent of your policy's death benefits in return for the right to the full benefits once you die. To qualify for any of these programs, you usually need your doctor to certify that your probable life expectancy is no more than six months to a year.

The drawback: your dependents don't receive the policy's death benefits when you die. If you're considering exercising this option, ask yourself if the need is dire enough to justify leaving your survivors without the financial safety net you envisioned. However, if you have no dependents, and you're out of money, cashing in on your life insurance may be your best option.

If you're healthy and thinking of buying a policy that offers living benefits, make sure that you first have adequate disability insurance. Receiving disability benefits can help you avoid the financial difficulties that a chronic or terminal illness can create.

☞ **The National Insurance Consumer Helpline (800-942-4242), a service sponsored by life-insurance trade groups, can answer additional questions you may have about living-benefits policies and tell you which companies offer them.**

6

Real-life
AUDITS

Three Personal Stories

F YOU'VE EVER CONSIDERED insurance a buy-and-forget product, think again. What kind and how much insurance you need depend on your stage of life, your responsibilities, and the assets you need to protect. Young singles have completely different insurance concerns than do middle-aged parents or the elderly.

Now that you know the basics, let's put it all together. To illustrate how real people handle their insurance needs, I've profiled three families who are at dramatically different stages of life: Brenda Rhodes is a single young woman who spends long hours running her own business. Anne and Bob Wharton are in their 40s and have three school-age daughters, a house, and all the accompanying responsibilities. And Charlie and Sybil Bittenbring are retired—enjoying their hobbies, community work, and family and

friends, and reviewing their own unique insurance requirements.

These stories serve as examples of how it pays to periodically reevaluate your insurance. Insurance reviews are especially important, of course, when you reach certain milestones. Buying a new car, getting a first job after graduation, getting married or divorced, having a baby, and reaching retirement are all events that should trigger a new look at your insurance portfolio. But insurance commands enough of your budget and resources to justify taking a comprehensive look at your portfolio every year or two and figuring out where you should beef up or reduce your coverage—and how you can save money on your premiums.

THE WHARTONS:
IN THE PRIME OF THEIR LIVES

ANNE AND BOB WHARTON of College Station, Texas, are the type of clients that an insurance agent dreams of. With one income, a mortgage, and three daughters— ages 17, 16, and 12—the couple needs all kinds of insurance and lots of it.

Bob, 48, is a professor of entomology at Texas A&M; Anne, 47, is a stay-at-home mom. Since they're about to begin writing college-tuition checks and will do so for several years, it's essential that the family have adequate life and disability insurance. Like all homeowners, they need to make sure their largest investment is covered in case of a fire or other disaster.

With two of their daughters now driving, the family's auto-insurance rates are probably the highest they'll ever be. And like most families, the Whartons, whose income is about $60,000, have to watch their budget carefully. Janet Briaud, the Bryan, Texas, fee-only financial planner who is the family's financial adviser, sums it up neatly: "Anne and Bob need the maximum insurance for the smallest dollars right now. Their biggest insurance expenses are occurring today. Their expenses will go down over the next 8 to 10 years, as their kids will be out of school and self-supporting."

How does their insurance portfolio measure up?

Auto insurance: A few years ago, the Whartons were paying about $1,200 a year in auto insurance on two vehicles. Today their premiums are nearly $2,800 a year, thanks to the addition of Pipit, 17, and Tara, 16, to the family's auto-insurance coverage. The couple has two vehicles: a 1991 Mitsubishi pickup truck with 37,000 miles on it, which Bob regularly uses, and a 1994 Mercury Tracer station wagon, also with 37,000 miles on it, that Anne and the girls usually drive.

Currently, the Whartons have a State Farm auto-insurance policy with 100/300/50 liability coverage. That means that their insurance would pay a maximum of $100,000 for each person injured, up to a limit of $300,000, and for $50,000 of property damage, in any accident they might cause.

Those are fairly standard coverage levels. All states have minimum mandated levels, and like many states, Texas sets low ones: it requires $20,000 in bodily-injury liability insurance, up to $40,000 per accident, and $15,000 of property-damage liability. These limits would leave the Whartons dangerously exposed to liability suits. "If you had an accident and totaled someone's Lexus, you'd know that $50,000 is not too much to carry in property-damage liability," says Briaud.

The Whartons also have uninsured motorist coverage, in the same amounts: 100/300/50. That means that if someone who is driving around with no insurance hit them, they'd be covered.

The Whartons currently carry collision and comprehensive insurance, with a deductible of $250 for collisions and $50 for theft or damages that aren't a result of an accident. That means their insurer would pay to fix their car if it were damaged or stolen, except for the first $250 (or $50) in repairs.

Anne and Bob take advantage of some money-saving discounts available from State Farm. Because they have both auto and homeowners insurance with the firm and they have been policyholders for several years, they get a discount of about $100 a year. The automatic seat belts on the Mercury earn them a $10 discount, and the driver's training classes their daughters have taken save them $132 a year. And since the couple have clean driving records, they've already locked in additional savings on their premium.

RECOMMENDATIONS: The Whartons should look hard at two money-saving strategies: raising their deductibles and taking the collision and comprehensive coverage off their cars.

The Mercury Tracer is new enough that it wouldn't be wise to take the collision off. But the 1991 Mitsubishi truck deserves closer scrutiny: although it doesn't have high mileage, it's an older car. The best way to decide whether to take collision off is to find out what the book value of the car is. If the vehicle was totaled, State Farm would reimburse the Whartons only up to the book value. If this was only $2,000, for example, it would clearly make sense to drop the coverage, for which the family is now paying about $200.

Anne Wharton, who handles the family's insurance matters, found out that the book value of the car is actually $6,375. Her call: keep the collision. Wharton also decided to keep deductibles at their relatively low level. The next step up is $500 for collision and $250 for other than collision. Raising deductibles would save $205 a year and makes a certain amount of sense, but Anne doesn't feel comfortable doing that. "Because this is a college town, there is an incredibly high rate of fender benders," she says.

Homeowners insurance: The Whartons pay $559 a year for homeowners insurance on their 19-year-old, 2,200-square-foot suburban home, which provides $98,500 of protection on the dwelling and $59,100 on their personal property. Since their home is inside a flood zone, they also have flood insurance through a federal program for an additional $283 a year.

Their daughters are avid musicians, so the family has an all-perils rider for $16,000 of coverage on the cello, flute, and viola that their daughters play. That rider, which adds about $85 a year to their home-owners policy, replaces a much more expensive policy they had a few years ago. "We had musical-instrument insurance through a company that offers it as a stand-alone policy. But it wasn't an all-peril policy, and in order to collect, the instrument had to be stolen or vandalized," says Anne Wharton.

Since the instruments get carried back and forth to school and to concerts around the state, they could easily be damaged in any number of ways. Moreover, coverage for the cello alone cost about $100 a year. Adding a rider to their existing policy bought them more coverage for less.

RECOMMENDATIONS: Increase insurance on the family's home and possessions.

"People should look at their dwelling from the standpoint of what it would cost to rebuild it," says Janet Briaud. "It has nothing to do with what you could sell it for and nothing to do with what you bought it for. Look at what new building costs are for a house of a similar size. If you had a fire, the cost to take down Sheetrock and rebuild and remodel is more than if you started over fresh."

The same is true for the personal-property insurance. "It's not that the value of your belongings is so high, but the cost to replace everything—all your clothing, furniture, and appliances—would be high. There are things you've accumulated over the years that you don't even realize you've accumulated," Briaud says.

Briaud is keenly aware of the dangers of underinsuring a home. She saw a neighbor suffer a substantial loss when his home burned three years ago. "He had bought it in 1990 and insured it for what he had paid for it," she says, "but it cost more to rebuild. After the fire, the structure of his house was fine, but he was out something like $50,000 on the dwelling and almost as much on personal property. After seeing that, I increased my own insurance," she says.

In the Whartons' community, estimated rebuilding costs are about $50 to $60 a square foot; so the 2,200-square-foot house should be insured for $110,000 to $132,000. Personal property should be insured for at least 60 percent of the replacement value of the house, or about $79,000. Increasing coverage to these levels will only cost an extra $65 a year. The Whartons are considering doing this.

Health insurance: The Whartons' health insurance, like that of most families, is provided by an employer—in this case, Texas A&M, where Bob teaches. Three years ago, the university switched to a health plan that requires employees to choose between a health maintenance organization (HMO) and a preferred provider organization (PPO). The Whartons chose the PPO.

Texas A&M pays $363 of the family's $450 monthly premium; Bob and Anne pay the rest. The coverage has a $400 annual deductible that applies to expenses such as hospitalization, out-patient surgery, and tests like mammograms. If the family stays in the PPO's network of physicians and providers, its costs are low indeed: the copayment on doctor visits is typically $10. If they stray out of the network, however, costs are higher: the annual deductible is $800, and even after that is satisfied, only 60 percent of a physician's bill is covered.

Texas A&M's health policy has an appropriate annual out-of-pocket cap: $1,200 per individual and $2,400 per family. Once medical bills exceed that, a higher level of coverage kicks in. And the university's lifetime maximum is $2 million. "A lot of plans still only have $1 million, and I don't think it's enough," says Janet Briaud. "If you have someone with some catastrophic problems, $1 million can add up pretty fast, especially for a whole family. I always tell people to talk to their employer and urge them to increase the coverage to $2 million."

The family pays for its own dental insurance, $53.40 a month. That coverage makes sense only because the Whartons had high dental bills in years past. In 1995 they made ample use of their dental coverage. There were 10 teeth cleanings, 3 crowns, 1 set of braces, and "a cavity filled here or there."

One important employee benefit that the Whartons take advantage of: the university's flexible-spending plan, which allows them to pay medical bills using pre-tax dollars. Anne Wharton set aside $160 a month in their "taxsaver" account in 1995 and used the reserve to pay for items such as glasses, contact lenses, dental work, and orthodontist visits. Last year's tax savings were an estimated $432.

RECOMMENDATIONS: Switch to an HMO and raise the contribution to the flexible-spending account.

The family could cut its health-insurance premiums by more than $40 a month by signing up with an HMO. But Anne prefers having the choice of physicians that the PPO offers. As for the flexible-spending account, the Whartons are planning to increase their contribution this year.

Disability insurance: Bob is covered by a long-term disability policy from UNUM Life Insurance Co., a major disability insurer, offered by Texas A&M. Since Anne isn't working outside the home, disability insurance isn't available to her. The policy—on which Bob pays the entire $15 monthly premium so that if he ever receives benefits, they will be tax-free— specifies that if he's disabled, after a 60-day waiting period, he'll get 65 percent of his salary.

It is an own-occupation policy that converts to an any-occupation policy after five years. So, within the first five years, if Bob's unable to perform his own job, he'll get benefits; after that he won't collect unless he's unable to perform any job for which he's qualified by education and experience. The policy does provide residual benefits, which means that even if he goes back to work part-time, he can claim a percentage of his benefits. Short-term disability would be covered by the sick days he is allowed to accrue in his job.

RECOMMENDATIONS: Investigate private insurance if Bob changes jobs or Anne goes back to work.

The Whartons are adequately covered now, but one of the drawbacks of having a group disability policy is that it isn't portable. If Bob switched jobs or careers he'd be dropped from the policy and have to find his own disability insurance. He's in perfect health now, but if that changed he'd pay prohibitive rates for private coverage.

"Bob couldn't buy private insurance without canceling this policy, because you can't duplicate coverage on the policies," says Briaud. "It's hard to argue that he should give up a $15-a-month policy to replace it with one that is going to cost him $200 a month. He's in good health and good condition. If money wasn't a concern, maybe we'd do a private policy. But money is a concern, and I think it's tough to justify."

Briaud's real worry is what could happen to Bob after 65: his coverage ends at age 65, and if he had become disabled earlier, he would have stopped contributing to his retirement plan. "He'd have Social Security then, but you can't count much on it," says Briaud. "They'll need more than just Social Security." The couple's contingency plan is for Anne, who has a master's degree in teaching, to go back to work if Bob is incapacitated.

Life insurance: Anne doesn't have life insurance. Bob has a USAA annual-renewable term (ART) life policy worth $147,745, costing about $400 a year.

RECOMMENDATIONS: Dramatically increase Bob's life insurance.

With a family income in the $60,000 range, and given the couple's monthly expenses and the fact that they have three daughters to put through college, they need an additional $250,000 in coverage. The good news is that the policy they have—annual-renewable term, bought through USAA, a no-commission, low-cost insurance company based in San Antonio—is a smart choice. USAA has top-notch financial ratings, and with an ART plan the Whartons are getting the most insurance for a low annual cost. They hope that as their daughters grow to adulthood, their financial obligations ease, and their personal assets increase, they will be able to cut back or drop their life insurance.

In choosing what type of additional coverage to get, Anne spoke with USAA. The company offers additional term coverage in two ways—with level premiums over 10 years and with increasing premiums. (Term life-insurance premiums generally increase each year as the insured gets older and is more likely to die.) The USAA representative made level term sound pretty attractive, contrasting its 10-year cost of $7,475 for an additional $250,000 of coverage with premiums of $9,715 for increasing term. So why does Briaud think the increasing-premium policy would be better?

For a couple of reasons. "With level premiums, you're overpaying in the early years," points out Briaud. "Also I doubt whether those figures take into account the present value of the money that you pay early. That would make those two figures a great deal closer indeed. Also the 10-year level premium locks you in. We don't know what's going to happen over 10 years, whether you'll still need and want insurance."

Another drawback: with this particular policy, at the end of the 10-year period you have to reenter the insurance pool, and if your health has declined, you may be in a more expensive class. It helps to look at insurance pragmatically. Most insurance policies are dropped after three or four years. If you've overpaid in the early years and then you drop or switch your policy, those dollars are lost.

Anne also checked with Texas A&M and found that as an employee, Bob could purchase additional life insurance through the university at even cheaper rates. For $432 a year, they can buy $240,000 of extra insurance on his life. (The maximum coverage is four times his annual salary.) By contrast, the USAA policy costs $648 a year for $250,000 in insurance. An additional perk for Bob Wharton: the university policy doesn't require a physical, only a questionnaire. Bob hasn't had any health problems, but with his busy schedule, bypassing a physical is appealing and makes the whole process easier. The policy is written by Metropolitan Life, which has a top-flight rating from the ratings agencies.

Verdict: the Whartons decided to purchase the Texas A&M policy.

Should Anne have life insurance? If money were not an issue, yes. One common mistake families make is underestimating what it would cost to replace a stay-at-home mom. But coverage is most needed when children are young and would require some sort of full-time day care. The Whartons probably should have insured Anne in years past, but with their daughters that are now 12, 16, and 17, insuring her is not so critical, particularly considering the family's tight budget.

Other insurance: Do Anne and Bob Wharton need umbrella liability insurance? You'll recall that umbrella liability is a broad-based policy, designed to kick in and provide coverage if you're sued and the costs and awards exceed your regular auto- or homeowners-insurance limits. Coverage of $1 million is highly desirable and not terribly expensive. But Janet Briaud makes a good argument that the Whartons don't need such a policy.

"You have to look at what assets they have if someone is trying to sue them," she says. "In Texas, they can't garnish your wages, your house is protected by law, and your retirement-plan assets are protected by law." Given those facts, the Whartons don't have a lot of vulnerable assets.

Briaud, however, does suggest that Anne and Bob look into a more unusual policy: long-term-care insurance for their parents. "I always ask my clients: How are your parents? Do they have enough money or might they need your help?"

In some cases, if it appears that someone is going to have to pay for nursing-home care for their parents, buying a long-term-care policy for them might be prudent. For the Whartons, it's unnecessary, since their parents have enough assets to cover their own costs for the foreseeable future. But as with all insurance needs, Anne and Bob Wharton plan to periodically review this potential gap.

WHARTON RECAP

- ◆ Beef up homeowners insurance
- ◆ Boost the amount stashed away in a flexible-spending account for medical bills
- ◆ Add $250,000 of annual-renewable term life insurance on Bob
- ◆ Skip umbrella liability insurance and long-term-care coverage for their parents for now
- ◆ Review auto-insurance needs as their teenagers leave home

BRENDA RHODES:
A YOUNG SOLE PROPRIETOR

AT 31, BRENDA RHODES HAS already been a small-business owner for eight years. She was just a year out of college, and working for a man who had a cosmetics business, when she decided to be her own boss. "I thought to myself, I could do this," says Rhodes. With the confidence and energy that characterizes both the young and the entrepreneurial, she canvassed friends and acquaintances about what kinds of businesses they might recommend. Rhodes settled on a typesetting business. Her parents cosigned a loan for $46,000 to buy the necessary equipment, and she set up Express Typesetting.

"I was very young," she says, "it never occurred to me that I could fail. In the beginning it was hard, but by the second year I was making money."

As a small-business owner, Rhodes has some special insurance needs. One of the dubious distinctions of being your own boss is that you have to be your own benefits manager, so Rhodes has had to buy her own individual health and disability insurance. In addition to being a business owner, Rhodes is single and childless and so requires a different insurance portfolio than someone with dependents. The specifics:

Auto insurance: Because Rhodes lives in New Jersey, which perennially tops the lists of the most expensive states in the United States for automobile insurance, her bills are higher than they would be in many other parts of the country. She does have her age and her gender going for her, however. All other things being equal, were she a young, single man under the age of 25, she'd pay about $340, or about 20 percent more, for the coverage she currently has.

As it is, her insurance isn't cheap. For her 1989 Toyota Camry, she pays $820.73 every six months

($1,641.46 a year) to provide herself with liability coverage of $100,000/$300,000/$50,000 from Hanover Insurance Co. That means if she has an accident, she's covered for bodily injury of $100,000 per person, up to a per-accident limit of $300,000, and for $50,000 in property damage. These are standard limits, and going lower, as state minimums will permit, isn't advisable.

Rhodes also has collision and comprehensive coverage on her car, with low deductibles: $250 for collision and $100 for comprehensive. That portion of the coverage costs her $287 of her total six-month premium. In addition, she has personal-injury protection coverage, which is required by New Jersey state law. It covers expenses and provides coverage, income continuation of $175 a week, up to a maximum of $18,200, if she's unable to work, and funeral benefits of $2,000. That package accounts for $107 of her premium.

Rhodes gets two discounts on her policy: one for having passive restraints on her car and one for choosing to limit her ability to sue in case of an accident. The "lawsuit threshold" effective in her state prescribes when she can sue someone for pain, suffering, and inconvenience. Brenda would have to suffer death or serious injury, such as dismemberment, significant disfigurement, or permanent loss of a body part, before she or her heirs could sue. "The threshold basically eliminates the soft-tissue injuries like whiplash, which are difficult to prove or disprove," says Diahann W. Lassus, the New Providence, New Jersey, CPA and fee-only planner who is Brenda's financial adviser.

RECOMMENDATIONS: Increase her deductibles to $500 for collision and $250 for comprehensive.

That simple move could save Rhodes $72 a year. Rhodes's auto-insurance premiums are running higher than average for her age and the make of her car. In part this is because she has "points" on her driving record for speeding tickets. Points stay on a record for three years. If the next few years pass without additional violations, Rhodes should check with her insurance agent to make sure those surcharges come off her record and bills as they expire.

But the higher premiums also reflect the very low deductibles she's chosen for her collision and comprehensive. The current book value of her car is about $8,000, which rules out dropping collision and comprehensive altogether. Still, she should keep an eye on depreciation and consider dropping collision once the car's value dips below about $2,000.

Rhodes has a good relationship with her insurance agent, who is a personal friend. After a small accident a few years ago, she called her agent, discussed it, and decided not to file a claim. "My damages were estimated at $1,250, and my insurance would have gone up $500 a year for the next three years, so it wasn't worth it," she says.

Recently, Rhodes moved to a different apartment, which is located closer to her office, and she took care to notify her insurer. Since how far a driver has to travel to work is one of the factors that helps determine auto-insurance rates, Rhodes qualified for a lower rate and received a refund of $41 on her six-month premium.

Renters insurance: Rhodes, like many young singles, rents an apartment with a friend. Neither of the women has renters insurance.

RECOMMENDATIONS: Buying renters coverage should be a priority.

This is an important hole in Rhodes's financial affairs. Though her personal possessions are minimal, it would be expensive to replace everything at once. But the big concern is her liability exposure.

"If somebody trips on your rug and sues you and you don't have liability insurance, they can go after your personal assets," points out Lassus. Whether or not her roommate obtains coverage is immaterial; Rhodes needs it for herself.

The New Jersey Dept. of Insurance regularly publishes premium-comparison surveys. For Rhodes's county, a tenants policy with $15,000 in contents and $100,000 in liability coverage and a $250 deductible averages $104 a year. She probably would want more coverage than that, since she estimates that her personal belongings are worth more than $15,000. "I have a microwave and VCR and jewelry and all sorts of things like that," says Rhodes.

A policy providing $25,000 of contents and $300,000 of liability coverage, would cost only approximately $150 a year. An umbrella liability policy that would provide up to $1 million in coverage is also advisable and would also cost $150. The additional $300 a year for both coverages would not only reimburse Rhodes for her destroyed or stolen belongings but also provide the all-important liability coverage she lacks.

Disability insurance: Unlike many young singles, Rhodes has disability insurance, purchased six years ago at the urging of her insurance agent. "Young people, especially single people, tend not to look at how expensive it is for them to live and the fact that their expenses are not going to go away if they're disabled," says Lassus. "And business owners often say, 'Well, I'd have to be totally disabled before I wouldn't be able to work.' But the reality is that even a short disability can be devastating."

Because she is a business owner, Rhodes has two policies. One covers her business overhead for a limited period of time. These premiums are tax deductible as a business expense. "Coverage like this will enable her to continue to pay rent and employees and the basic expenses of her business so it could stay open even though she isn't there," says Lassus.

Rhodes also has disability insurance to cover her personal expenses, which are minimal. Her current coverage would pay her about $4,000 monthly for business overhead and about $1,000 a month for personal disability. The policy costs about $1,200 a year, has a 30-day waiting period before benefits kick in, provides residual benefits, and would cover her for five years.

RECOMMENDATIONS: Increase the waiting period and extend the life span of her personal coverage.

Rhodes's business-overhead disability coverage is adequate, but her personal disability needs to be increased, probably to $2,000 a month. At the same time, she should lengthen the waiting period before the policy would take effect to 60 or even 180 days. She's been able to beef up her savings in recent years, so the waiting period she needed six years ago, when she bought the policy, doesn't apply anymore. "I have more now than I did when I was 25," she says.

The fact that Rhodes is covered for only five years is a problem. Certainly, if she couldn't return to her business for five years, she'd probably close or sell it. But her need for personal coverage would continue. Rhodes needs to try to find coverage that extends, even at a reduced rate, to age 65.

Health insurance: In New Jersey, individuals who are in the market for health insurance can purchase one of four traditional indemnity policies or coverage from an HMO. In 1994 the state began requiring insurers to offer exactly the same coverage in each category, with the A plans offering the most limited benefits and the E plans the most comprehensive ones. This makes it easy to comparison shop, which Rhodes has done. Her current coverage is through a traditional fee-for-service policy, which allows her to use whichever physicians and hospitals she chooses. Her deductible is $1,000 a year, and she is reimbursed for 80 percent of her bills, up to a limit of $2,000 a year. After that, the insurer—Celtic Life Insurance Co.—will pay 100 percent of bills. There is no lifetime maximum on her benefits, and prescriptions are covered. Her premiums are $160 a month.

RECOMMENDATIONS: Shop the market every year when the policy comes up for renewal. Though an HMO would cut her costs, at this point she'd be required to change doctors, which she's opposed to.

Although Rhodes was dismayed when the new plan took effect and her deductible rose from $100 to $1,000 a year, this policy fits the bill of providing good coverage in the case of a serious illness or injury and catastrophic bills. Paying $1,000 in medical expenses before her coverage takes effect is affordable for her. But she should still look around at renewal time: since comparison shopping is easier after New Jersey's health-insurance reforms, the market is likely to be competitive.

Life insurance: Rhodes is single and has no dependents, so she has no great need for life insurance. But she does have one concern that she wants addressed should she die: When she started her business, her parents cosigned an equipment loan she took out. If she died, she would want the existing balance on that loan paid off so her parents wouldn't have to worry about it. The balance is approximately $19,000, so Rhodes has a $25,000 whole-life policy, purchased four years ago from Guardian, for which she pays an annual premium of $276. The existing cash balance is $407.

"As soon as I pay the bill, I send it right to my mother. She's the beneficiary, not me," says Rhodes, "and if anything happened to me, she'd be able to find what she needed right away." Since she's 31 and in good health, disaster is not likely, but she's thoughtfully saved her beneficiaries from the agonizing experience of hunting for the proper documents while grieving the loss of a loved one.

RECOMMENDATIONS: Revisit her insurance needs if her life and responsibilities change, and if she needs additional coverage, purchase term insurance, not more whole life.

Rhodes is wise enough to know exactly what she needs life insurance for, and she bought it for that specific purpose. Too many consumers buy life insurance on the vague recommendation of an agent that "someday you'll need it." Though she won't always have that specific need—a business loan that her parents share responsibility for—Rhodes figures that even if she never has dependents, she will want a minimal life-insurance policy in effect to pay what's euphemistically called "final expenses": a decent burial and any small debts that may be left when she dies. Since she's her own employer, she lacks the life insurance that is often provided as a part of a larger company's benefits package: the one- or two-times salary coverage.

If Rhodes were making a life-insurance purchase now, we'd push term insurance. According to a premium survey done by the New Jersey Dept. of Insurance, a 30-year-old woman buying $100,000 of term in that state pays an average of $173 a year. Rhodes, of course, is paying $276 a year, for $25,000 of death benefits. The argument for term: prices go up, but it would take a long time for the premium even to begin to approach Rhodes's. At age 50, term insurance for $100,000 in death benefits is still only $412 a year. By the time she reached that age, Rhodes could have built up enough assets not to need insurance to cover final expenses.

But since she's owned her current policy for four years, she's passed the early—and most expensive—years of paying top-dollar commissions and is now poised to accumulate a small cash value in the policy. Guardian is top-rated by each of the rating agencies and paid a respectable 8.5 percent in dividends last year, so it's reasonable for Rhodes to hold on to the policy.

However, should she decide to buy more insurance, she should definitely buy term, not whole life. What would be good reasons to get additional coverage? If somewhere down the line, Rhodes was financially contributing to her parents' support, she might want to think about more insurance. About the only other reason would be if she wanted to make a bequest to a favorite charity upon her death. "Some people feel very strongly they want their name to live on after they die, and they want to make a charitable gift," says Lassus. "A term-insurance policy is a cheap way to do that."

RHODES RECAP

◆ Increase auto-insurance deductibles to $500 for collision and $250 for comprehensive. Keep an eye on the blue-book value of her Toyota Camry. When it drops below $2,000, drop collision and comprehensive. Also, keep track of when her speeding points expire, and make sure her auto-insurance premiums drop accordingly

◆ Buy renters insurance for personal property and liability. Start shopping by calling the companies offering the four or five lowest-priced policies mentioned in the New Jersey insurance department's renters-premium survey

◆ Add another $2,000 a month in disability-insurance benefits; add coverage to age 65 at a reduced level

CHARLIE AND SYBIL BITTENBRING:
PARED-DOWN NEEDS

IN THEIR RETIREMENT, Charles and Sybil Bittenbring, 76 and 74, keep a schedule that is as busy as it was during their working years. Charlie volunteers with the Boy Scouts, his local church, and as AARP Virginia president, while Sybil is a volunteer with the Kennedy Center for the Arts in Washington, D.C. In the summer, they give away bags of fresh vegetables from their abundant garden to friends and neighbors. Between them, the couple have six children and eight grandchildren. The Bittenbrings, both of whom lost previous spouses, met and married 18 years ago, when they were employed by the Navy.

The two are fairly well-off: they have civil-service and military pensions (Sybil's deceased husband was also military), as well as Social Security and income from the assets they've spent a lifetime working hard to accumulate. Since retiring in 1983, they've barely slowed down, but their insurance needs have changed dramatically. The specifics:

Automobile insurance: The couple own three vehicles—a 1995 Chrysler New Yorker, a 1989 Plymouth Horizon, and a 1981 Chevrolet pickup truck that Charlie uses primarily for scouting activities. The Bittenbrings are insured with USAA, a San Antonio–based direct marketer of insurance that sells primarily to military officers and their families. The couple has liability coverage of $300,000/$500,000 for bodily injury (the first limit refers to how much the company will pay out for injuries for any one passenger, the second to the total for all passengers in any single accident), as well as $50,000 for property-damage liability and $5,000 for medical-payments insurance. They have the same amount of coverage for uninsured or underinsured motorists. The Bittenbrings also carry collision and comprehensive on their vehicles, with a deductible of $100. Their annual premium runs about $1,250 for coverage on all three vehicles.

Many seniors see auto premiums go up after age 65, but the Bittenbrings, who have good driving records and no recent history of accidents and claims, have been largely unaffected. A few years ago Charlie Bittenbring took the "55 Alive" defensive-driving course that AARP offers to seniors. Upon completing it he called USAA to ask about a discount on his premium and was told by the person he spoke with, "You already enjoy our lowest rate and are not eligible for any additional discounts."

Bittenbring let the matter drop. Later his wife took such a course, and he called back to inquire again about the discounts. This time he was armed with the knowledge that the state of Virginia requires insurers to give discounts to policyholders who have completed such a course. He finally scored a victory, obtaining a discount—one half of a percent of the premium, but a discount nonetheless.

RECOMMENDATIONS: At $100, the couple's auto-insurance deductible is unnecessarily low. "I think you can take a common-sense approach to a deductible," David Drucker, a Bethesda, Maryland, fee-only financial planner, told them. "If you have ample savings, as you do, you can go with a higher deductible."

Charlie Bittenbring agreed, and plans to investigate increasing the deductible to $250 or even to $500. "To tell you the truth, until I got out my policy and looked, I really did think I had a $250 deductible," he says. Increasing the deductible could save the Bittenbrings an estimated $75 a year on their premium.

Another smart move: consider dropping collision and comprehensive on the truck and perhaps on the 1989 Plymouth, both of which are old enough to have decreased in value. The potential savings to the couple: more than $100.

The Bittenbrings' insurer, USAA, is known as a lower-cost provider, since it sells policies directly by telephone and doesn't incur the extra costs of an agent system. Charlie has had two claims paid by USAA over the years and was happy with how both were handled.

Homeowners insurance: The couple own their home in northern Virginia and two rental properties—a condominium and a single-family home in Florida. The homeowners insurance on their primary residence, as well as on the single-family home they rent out, is from USAA. The condominium insurance is provided through the couple's condo fees.

Their 3,000-square-foot Virginia home is insured for $175,000, and personal property is covered for 75 percent of that. Seniors should be particularly alert to how much they have in personal-property insurance, since they have spent years accumulating valued belongings. A couple in their 60s are more likely to be under-insured for personal property than two 30-year-olds.

For several years, Sybil Bittenbring has wisely carried additional coverage on personal belongings through a separate policy for which she pays about $250 a year. The coverage is on scheduled valuables, such as jewelry and silverware, that exceed the main policy's limits.

"Someone could walk into the house and just take the silver chest," she says. She had occasion to make use of her coverage when one of her rings lost a stone not long ago.

"A lot of people don't realize they don't have full coverage under their regular homeowners," says Drucker.

The Bittenbrings are due to have their homeowners policy updated; they're in the process of adding a deck and a screened porch to their home. USAA, like most insurers, requires owners to notify it if they add more than $5,000 or 5 percent to the value of their house, so that the insured amount can be increased accordingly.

It's especially important that the face value of the Bittenbrings' homeowners policy be high enough to pay for rebuilding if the home is lost, since face value is what determines the cap on the amount the insurer will pay. USAA's homeowners policy specifies that the company will pay up to 150 percent of face value if the insured's home is lost. Some firms don't put a cap on the guaranteed replacement-cost coverage. The Bittenbrings' 3,000-square-foot home is insured for $175,000. The most USAA would reimburse the couple for rebuilding costs would be $262,500 (150 percent of $175,000), which works out to $87.50 a square foot. That's pretty close to actual rebuilding costs in the northern Virginia suburb where they live.

The Bittenbrings' rental home has dwelling coverage for standard hazards, such as fire, windstorm, and hail. Since the furnishings are all owned by the tenants, the couple doesn't have personal-property insurance on that house.

Charlie and Sybil Bittenbring do have a significant gap in their homeowners insurance. Although they have fairly standard liability coverage of $300,000, they do not have an umbrella liability policy.

RECOMMENDATIONS: Increase homeowners coverage to take into account the local rebuilding costs and include the new addition the couple are building on their home. Check local rebuilding costs to pinpoint the accuracy of their homeowners coverage. Increase the deductible on the homeowners policy from the current $100 level to $250 or $500.

Get an umbrella liability policy. In the Bittenbrings' case, this is a serious oversight. Over their lifetimes, they have accumulated assets that could make an attractive target in a lawsuit.

"Homeowners insurance has liability coverage of perhaps $300,000," says David Drucker, "but with inflation and higher net worth, people want more liability coverage. An umbrella liability policy gives you additional coverage over a standard homeowners and auto policy. If you get them all from the same company, they can be totally interlocking—all the coverages have the same dates, and you can be assured that there are no gaps and no overlapping sections where you're paying for double coverage."

An umbrella liability policy on top of their homeowners from USAA would cost approximately $300 a year for $1 million of coverage. This is an expenditure well worth making.

Sybil Bittenbring is also overdue to have her personal property appraised to make sure she has it adequately covered. She might also want to check whether coverage might come at a lower price as a rider to the existing USAA policy rather than through a separate stand-alone policy.

Health insurance: The couple are eligible for Medicare, as are most U.S. citizens over the age of 65. But there are notable gaps in this coverage, and many seniors find they need Medicare-supplemental insurance if they are not covered under some sort of retiree health-insurance program.

As a retired military officer, Charlie Bittenbring has full medical-insurance coverage from the federal government. Sybil Bittenbring also qualifies for the coverage. However, as Charlie points out, routine medical care is not always readily available from the military providers.

"What a lot of people don't realize is that medical benefits for retired military are on a 'space available' basis," he says. "If I were to have a heart attack right

now, they'd send me in an ambulance over to Bethesda, and they'd take good care of me. But if I were to
go over there this afternoon with a sore throat and
want to see a doctor, I'd sit maybe four hours and
then maybe see a doctor or maybe a nurse."

After his retirement from the military, Charlie put
in another 13 years in the civil service. Sybil also had
several years of government service.

"When we retired from civil service, we had the
option of keeping our federal employees health-ben-
efit plan, for which the government pays the majority
of the premium," says Charlie. The Bittenbrings had
to make an irrevocable election: Charlie elected out
of the system ("I thought, I don't need that—I'm military," he says), while Sybil decided to hold on to her
insurance. A few years later, Charlie regretted his decision. Luckily, his wife was able to add him to her plan
as a spouse. The couple paid about $50 a month each
for their coverage, which picked up many of the
expenses that a typical Medicare-supplemental policy
would cover.

In January 1996 Charlie joined a local Medicare
HMO run by Humana and dropped the spousal coverage. "They are marketing heavily in this area," he says.

The advantages to him: he saves the $50 monthly
fee for his coverage under Sybil's plan and pays only
$5 each time he sees his doctor. Charlie's regular
physician happened to be affiliated with the HMO, so
the switch didn't involve finding another doctor. Bittenbring has been happy with his choice thus far, but
it is comforting for him to know that if he decides he
doesn't like it, he can always go back to regular
Medicare and then reenroll on his wife's policy.

"I've been pleased with it, although it may not be
for everyone," says Charlie. Sybil prefers to stay on regular Medicare, with her retiree plan providing the
supplemental coverage she needs.

RECOMMENDATIONS: The couple is lucky to have what is, effectively, duplicate coverage available to them. Medicare provides their first line of insurance. Sybil continues to pay about $50 a month for what amounts to Medicare-supplemental insurance as part of her civil-service retiree benefits. Charlie, since joining a Medicare HMO a few months ago, no longer pays for that. They also have underlying coverage available to them as a retired military family. "We feel fortunate," says Charlie Bittenbring.

Charlie is also lucky that his wife's coverage allows him to try out a managed Medicare program and then reenroll in her plan if he isn't satisfied. Currently, managed Medicare is being aggressively sold to seniors across the country. One selling point is that consumers can forgo Medicare-supplemental policies because the managed companies provide wider coverage than the ordinary Medicare program.

But experts urge seniors who have a private Medicare-supplement policy to hold on to it for a few months until they feel certain they're satisfied with the HMO. Once you cancel a supplemental Medicare policy, it can be difficult to buy another if you've developed health problems.

Life insurance: Between them, Charlie and Sybil have several paid-up cash-value life-insurance policies.

Beginning when he was in his 20s, Charlie Bittenbring began accumulating cash-value policies. He has an Equitable policy that has a cash value of about $2,400, a Metropolitan Life policy with a value of about $3,500, a $10,000 policy from USAA, a $10,000 policy from the Armed Forces Benefits organization, a policy currently worth $25,000 from Navy Mutual Aid, and a $50,000 policy from Massachusetts Mutual. Charlie also took out a life-insurance policy on himself for each of his children, which they own and are responsible for.

Sybil has a few paid-up life-insurance policies, too: $60,000 in policy coverage, as well as the $10,000 coverage each of the Bittenbrings has as a retirement benefit. Charlie's policies add up to about $100,000 in coverage, and Sybil's to about $70,000.

RECOMMENDATIONS: "There are two main reasons people have life insurance," says David Drucker. "One is for income replacement. That's when you have an obligation to another person, like a child or a spouse. As you get older, you save for your retirement in two ways: by investing discretionary income and by contributing to pension plans. Your need for income replacement drops." With their children grown and self-supporting, clearly Charlie and Sybil Bittenbring don't need to replace income.

"The other reason to have life insurance," says Drucker, "is, if you die with something illiquid in your estate, like a business or real estate that you don't want to sell to pay estate taxes, life insurance can provide the cash to pay those taxes." The Bittenbrings don't have assets that are particularly illiquid.

So, should they cash in their existing policies and invest the money elsewhere? "Should you continue carrying the life insurance since the policies are all paid up and not costing you anything out of pocket? The answer might be yes, but it's good to have all the facts," Drucker says. He suggests that people in this position analyze each policy to discover its investment return. "Sometimes, when you take into account dividends, these can be pretty good investments." Another issue to consider is how much tax the couple might have to pay if they cashed the policies in. Tax-protected exchanges are allowed for annuities under certain IRS regulations.

Sybil and Charlie have decided not to exchange or cash in their existing life-insurance policies. One reason is taxes. Some of the policies name their children as beneficiaries, and life-insurance death benefits are tax-free.

The couple also have emotional and psychological reasons. Over the years, Charlie and Sybil have each had the devastating experience of losing loved ones. Charlie was widowed with four young children, the youngest less than six months old. Sybil has been twice widowed and raised a daughter. They've developed an appreciation for how fragile life can be, and Sybil, especially, feels strongly that she wants to keep insurance policies in force. She feels it provides an extra cushion of stability for each of them and for their adult children.

This kind of financial-planning decision needs to take into account comfort level. "You can do the analysis, but I don't want to downplay peace of mind," says Drucker, "especially in a situation like this, where the policies are paid up and they are effectively costing you nothing. It's not worth all the time and aggravation and analysis if you're going to end up feeling badly about it."

Long-term-care insurance: None. Although Charlie and Sybil frequently get sales pitches for long-term-care policies from telemarketers and through stacks of junk mail, they have yet to bite.

RECOMMENDATIONS: The statistics cited to the couple by insurance salespeople are frightening—stories of $30,000-a-year nursing homes and the estimated percentage of seniors who will spend at least some time in one. However, on closer examination, the Bittenbrings aren't candidates for buying a policy.

"The danger of long-term care for a married couple is that one of you will need very expensive care and what has been one cost of living between the two of you will become two costs of living—one of them expensive," says Drucker. "You have to look at your savings and pensions. If that would deplete them rapidly or take you down to the poverty line, you need to consider long-term-care insurance. But if you run the numbers and have enough retirement income that it wouldn't happen, you may not need it."

The Bittenbrings' assets include their savings and their residence and rental properties, of course, but probably their most valuable are their guaranteed pensions. That income won't ever be diminished by depleted principal, will increase with inflation every year, and will keep coming whether or not they are in a nursing home. "There's nothing that beats an indexed pension from a stable income viewpoint," says Drucker. "That's as good as gold."

"We're fortunate," says Charlie Bittenbring. "Between our military retirement income and pensions and income, we could cover the cost of a nursing home. I thought very seriously about it. I thought about all the options of these policies—how large of a deductible to take and how long to take out insurance for, one year or three years or seven years. But I'm lucky. I don't want to be bothered with it, and I don't have to be."

BITTENBRING RECAP

◆ Raise auto and homeowners deductibles from $100 to at least $250

◆ Notify homeowners insurance company about the new addition being built on their home and increase homeowners coverage to include that, taking into consideration local rebuilding costs

◆ Have the personal property that is covered on a separate policy reappraised to ensure proper coverage, and perhaps consolidate coverage under USAA

◆ Buy an umbrella liability policy

CHAPTER 7

Making
CLAIMS

How to Get Satisfaction

YES, IT'S TRUE that the market for direct-response insurers—companies, like USAA and GEICO, that sell policies to the public via telephone—has exploded over the past two decades. It's also true that outlets like banks are gearing up to sell more insurance as the regulatory barriers that have traditionally prevented them from doing so are challenged. Not surprisingly, as competition from these other, more efficient distribution methods increases, the ranks of insurance agents are shrinking. The number of independent agencies is half of what it was in its heyday in the 1950s.

For many consumers, insurance agents are unnecessary. As we've discussed previously, it's often smarter for the self-motivated buyer to spend a little time and effort to purchase insurance through these other channels. In some

cases, agents are worse than unnecessary; they're harmful to your financial health. An example? The life-insurance agent who sells a consumer an inadequate cash-value policy rather than a higher-value term-life policy because the cash-value policy pays a higher commission to the agent.

But it would be a mistake to assume that insurance agents are going the way of the dinosaurs anytime soon. There are some 280,000 members of the Independent Insurance Agents of America, and the fact is that many consumers still feel more comfortable buying insurance through an agent. They may want someone who will make a house call or who they think will help battle an insurance claim, or they may have a trusted friend or relative who is in the business. And when an agent can coax a reluctant breadwinner to buy an adequate amount of life insurance, he or she is helping.

So what should you look for in an agent?

☞ **Comparison shop among independent agents and captive agents.**

There are two types of insurance agents: independent and captive insurance-company agents. Independent are self-employed and sell insurance for several companies. They are paid a commission on each policy sold. A captive agent (also called a direct writer or career agent) is employed by one company to sell its products. Companies like State Farm, Metropolitan Life, and Prudential are captive companies. A captive agent probably is commissioned but can be working on straight salary.

The obvious disadvantage of captive agents is that they sell only for their employer—if another company has a cheaper policy that would cover your needs, they're not going to tell you about it. The advantage of captive agents is that their commissions are often lower than independent agents', so a comparable policy can be cheaper.

An independent agent runs his or her own business and has agreements with several insurance companies to sell their policies. Therefore, the agent is free to shop the entire market for clients, hunting for the best policy at the best price. That's the theory, anyway.

But for independent agents, independence has limits. Most represent only approximately eight companies. There are practical financial reasons why they don't usually represent more. An insurer may require that an agent generate $350,000 a year in premium income for the company in order to continue representing it. An agent representing too many companies would never be able to meet all their required minimums. Big companies often offer indies incentives. Another policy or two written might qualify the agent for a bonus or a trip to Hawaii, for instance.

So the first thing you need to know about an agent is who he or she works for and answers to. When you're talking to an independent agent, ask how many companies the agency represents.

☞ **Look for an agent who has been in the business, full-time, for more than four years.**
According to a 1994 study done by the Life Insurance Marketing Research Association, only 17 percent of agents are still in the business after four years. Look for someone who has survived for at least that long.

☞ **Find an agent with the expertise you need.**
Many agents will specialize either in property/casualty insurance, which would include homeowners and auto insurance, or life, health, and disability insurance. If the agent doesn't deal regularly in the coverage you need, and if there isn't someone else in his or her agency that can advise you on that area, continue your search.

☞ **Look for advanced training in an area.**
All insurance agents have to be licensed by the state they do business in, but there are professional designations that indicate more extensive training, including a series of examinations on a particular subject. At the very least, these designations show the agent has made a commitment to the profession and has made an effort to become educated about the business and products. In addition to passing exams, candidates must have three years of practice under their belts, and they must participate in continuing-education programs.

The CLU, or chartered life underwriter, designation is the gold standard among life-insurance agents; the CPCU, or chartered property and casualty underwriter, applies to agents who sell homeowners and auto insurance. The RHU, or registered health underwriter, is a fairly new designation and is designed for those selling health insurance.

☞ **Steer clear of anyone who is in business part-time or as a hobby.**

You want someone who has the training, experience, and commitment to the business to give you top-notch service. A local football coach who sells insurance in the evening is unlikely to have the level of expertise and the time to represent you properly.

☞ **Trust your gut.**

Do you feel comfortable with the agent, and are you encouraged to ask questions? Does your agent make recommendations without asking you many questions? A good agent won't try to sell you coverage without discussing the particulars of your situation with you. Someone who fails to do that will probably try to sell you some sort of cookie-cutter policy that doesn't necessarily fit your needs. Is the agent willing to give you references—customers (not related by blood or marriage, preferably) whom you can contact to inquire whether they've been pleased with his or her service?

Like all businesses, the insurance industry has its share of incompetent and dishonest agents. Run, don't walk, away if your agent suggests it doesn't matter if you shade the truth on any medical questions. If the insurance company challenges your claim, saying that you were less than truthful when you applied, it's going to be tough to prove that your agent told you it didn't matter if you understated your weight by 30 pounds or described yourself as a nonsmoker.

Similarly, if your agent makes verbal promises about what is covered in a policy, follow up with a letter recounting your conversation and detailing his or her assurances. Send a copy to your agent and keep one yourself.

When you're talking to insurance agents, don't hesitate to tell them you're speaking with a couple of agents. I'd urge you to canvass both independent and captive agents, as well as a direct-response company, to comparison shop. And if you're in the market for cash-value life insurance, consider contacting a fee-only insurance adviser who can provide a sophisticated analysis of your needs without the bias that a commission can introduce. (See the "Fee-Only Advisers" box, page 167.) Be aware of the distinction between fee-only and fee-based advisers. The latter some-times do take commissions, a fact not always made clear to their clients.

10 QUESTIONS FOR INSURANCE AGENTS

1. What professional insurance designations have you earned?
2. How long have you been in this business?
3. How many companies do you represent?
4. Are you willing to disclose commissions?
5. Can you give at least five references from existing or former clients?
6. What kind of insurance do you specialize in?
7. How often do you review existing policies of clients?
8. Can you be reached after business hours and on weekends?
9. Have you ever been sued by a client or disciplined by the state insurance department?
10. When was the last time you earned continuing-education credits?

STAKING A CLAIM

BY DEFINITION, INSURANCE claim time is a distressing time for consumers—you've suffered a loss of some kind. "If someone steals my red Corvette, I'm still mad, whether I get paid or not," says Peter van Aartrijk, a spokesman for the Independent Insurance Agents of America. A survey done in 1994 by the IIAA found that 86 percent of consumers were satisfied with the way their insurance claims were handled. But with the huge numbers of claims filed every year, if even a small percentage of claimants are dissatisfied, there are plenty of policyholders out there who feel ill-served by the insurance industry.

Here are some simple guidelines to follow to help make the claims process go more smoothly.

ADVICE FROM CLAIMS-ASSISTANCE PROS

An estimated 8,000 claims-assistance professionals around the country charge hourly fees of anywhere from $25 to $100 to handle various jobs for clients. One of their services is interceding with insurance companies on behalf of patients who are having a tough time getting claims paid. Greta Tatken, director of Claims Recovery, a Burke, Virginia, claims-assistance firm, estimates that about 50 percent of the consumers who challenge denied claims are successful in getting additional payments. Often the challenge entails some detective work.

"A couple of years ago, a client of mine had a daughter who had surgery on her nose by an ENT specialist," says Tatken. "It wasn't plastic surgery; it was a type of reconstructive surgery. The insurance company didn't have a lot of experience with the procedure and wouldn't pay beyond a low usual, customary, and reasonable charge. The physician just billed the family for the balance. But after I submitted the operative notes, compared it to other similar procedures, and took a poll of what a couple of physicians in the area would charge, the insurer ended up paying in full."

If you need professional help with claims, try the National Association of Claims Assistance Professionals (NACAP) at 800-660-0665, or if you're on Medicare, ask your local senior-citizen agencies about free claims counseling. But for those who want to challenge their own medical claims, here are tactics suggested by the pros:

 **Know your policy.**

Agents report that one of the most unpleasant surprises consumers have to endure is realizing that they don't have the coverage they thought they did. Perhaps the homeowners policy a couple thought paid replacement value for their belongings really only covers actual cash value, so they get a pittance for their damaged eight-year-old, depreciated sofa.

◆ Enlist the help of your physician or provider. Sometimes a more detailed explanation of the services rendered will convince an insurer to pay. Other times the digits on a diagnosis code have been transposed or another simple error has been made.

◆ If your physician's office says it can't help, don't let the matter drop. "In doctor's offices, the person who answers the phone is often overworked and underpaid, and they won't take the initiative. If they tell you there's nothing you can do about it, write a letter to the physician. They're business owners, and this is a situation where you're not getting good service," says Tatken.

◆ If you are trying to battle a "usual, customary, and reasonable" fee denial, in which the insurer claims your physician charged too much, phone other providers in the area. If you tell them you are challenging such an insurance denial, most will gladly share fee information with you.

◆ Turn to the human resources department of your employer. "If it's a large corporation, there should be someone in that department whose job it is to help employees," says Tatken.

◆ If all else fails, go up the ladder at the insurance company or the HMO, to the firm's medical director, and then turn to the state insurance department. "Don't sue unless you've exhausted all other avenues," says Tatken.

Conversely, your policy may cover more than you think: something stolen from your car may be insured under your homeowners policy, for instance. Your auto policy may pay for a rental car while your car is in the shop after an accident. Knowing the specifics of your policy will enable you to reap the benefits of its coverage more fully. Consumers should also know what the deductible is on their homeowners-, auto-, and health-insurance policies.

Other policy provisions to make note of: How much time does the policy give you after an incident to file a claim—30 days, 90 days, or a year? What are your responsibilities after an accident or a loss? For instance, if a section of your home's roof blows off, you may well be required to take reasonable precautions to ensure that further damage doesn't occur. That may mean covering roof holes with a tarp to prevent rain damage or boarding up broken windows to prevent looting.

Your policy should also contain guidance on how to file a claim and what steps you have to take before filing. In an auto accident, you're probably required to tell the police and obtain a police report.

☞ Keep organized, impeccable records.
Make sure you know where your insurance policies are (preferably in a fireproof box in your home). Also keep paid receipts or canceled checks that prove you've paid your insurance premiums regularly. A bank safety-deposit box is not a good place to keep an insurance policy, particularly a life-insurance policy, since if you die, it is customarily sealed and cannot be easily accessed.

☞ Follow up a call with a letter and copies of all bills.
Even if you are entitled to phone in a claim, send a written account. Make copies of everything: claim forms, receipts, physician statements, and bills. For an auto claim, take photos of your car, the accident site, and any other relevant subjects. For a homeowners claim, take pictures of the damage, especially if you are seeking reimbursement for

temporary repairs. If your homeowners policy will cover your temporary living expenses, make sure you can document your hotel bills and other costs. Don't send originals of documents; send copies.

👉 **Use your home inventory to tally up your losses.**
In case you missed my earlier lecture on this subject, a recap: "The worst time to try to reconstruct what you have is when you've been traumatized by a fire and you're trying to remember," says IIAA's van Aartrijk. Take two hours out of your busy schedule, and walk around your house with a video camera. Describe the items you're taping, and talk about when and where you bought them and, if you can remember, how much you paid for them. (Copies of purchase receipts are even better.) Throw open your clothes closets and your kitchen cabinets, and film the insides, the better to remember how many sweaters you have and the infrequently used appliances you may otherwise overlook. Don't forget to tape the attic, the basement, and the garage, where you might stow expensive sports equipment or lawn and garden furnishings. Then stash the tape safely off-premises somewhere.

👉 **Keep a detailed log of all your conversations and your correspondence with the company in filing the claim.**
It will help if there are questions about the effort and steps you went through to try to settle the claim.

👉 **File your complaint promptly.**
Your insurance policy details how long you have to file a complaint. But don't wait until the deadline looms: not only will you remember the details about an incident better if you file promptly, but a long-delayed filing can make an insurance company suspicious. Chances are, if your insurer thinks it needs to sniff around for fraud, you'll wait longer for your check.

☞ Use your agent as a go-between if you feel the insurer's offer is too low.

Don't assume the insurance company's offer is final. A Louisiana man saw his five-year-old Honda Accura swamped when there was serious flooding in his town. Water seeped into the floorboard and destroyed the computers on the floor under the front seat that help the car run. Since it cost him $1,800 to replace the computers and he had a $500 deductible, he expected a check for $1,300.

But the insurer argued that since the car was five years old, the electronics had depreciated and reimbursed him only $500. "To say he was upset was an understatement," says Rick Katten, the man's New Orleans insurance agent. After Katten's pleading and cajoling, the company agreed to pay the difference.

The moral? The insurer's first offer may be negotiable. If you feel it is low—as it may well be—write to the company, detailing why you think you deserve a larger settlement. Buttress your position with repair estimates or an appraisal.

Still can't get satisfaction? Lean on your agent, if you use one. A good one can cite cases in which similar losses were fully covered and may be able to exert some influence with the company.

If you still can't come to an agreeable settlement, go up the ladder at your company. You can go to the supervisor, to its consumer complaint department, if it has one, or to the president or chief executive officer. Write letters patiently explaining the situation and why you think you have a legitimate case. Keep copies of all correspondence and a log of all telephone conversations.

☞ Use the state commissioner's office if you are still unhappy.

Most states have a procedure for investigating consumer complaints. Though they don't generally have the authority to force insurers to settle, sometimes just getting an inquiry from state regulators can spur a company to action. According to Audrey Selden, associate commissioner at the Texas

Dept. of Insurance, her office investigated nearly 21,000 complaints of all sorts in 1995 and through its intercession, succeeded in getting consumers $10.6 million in additional claims payments.

☞ **If you are going into binding arbitration, get a lawyer.**
The next step is some sort of dispute mediation or arbitration. Alternative dispute resolution (ADR) and arbitration involve bringing in outsiders, such as retired judges, to hear both sides of the story. In mediation, a middleman tries to find a middle ground that both sides can agree to. Arbitration is a more formal legal process and may well be binding: before starting the process both sides have to agree to abide by the final outcome, and the consumer has to agree not to file a subsequent lawsuit. A consumer going to binding arbitration should be represented by a lawyer.

The last step is to sue the insurance company. Exhaust all other possibilities first, since a lawsuit is going to cost you, in either per-hour lawyers' fees or contingency fees, calculated as a percentage of any award or settlement you get. If your claim is small, take a good look before you sue: a contingency attorney is unlikely to represent you on a $500 claim, and hourly fees may add up to more than the disputed amount.

If you do decide to sue, find an attorney who has experience representing plaintiffs in insurance suits. Check with your local bar association or call the American Bar Association (312-988-5000) for leads.

State
by State
GUIDE

MOST INSURANCE REGULATION TAKES place at the state, rather than the federal, level. That arrangement guarantees a crazy quilt of regulatory differences. Some states, for example, regulate how large a commission can be charged on certain types of policies—Medicare-supplemental or long-term-care—while others are strictly hands-off.

State insurance departments also publish information that can be valuable to consumers. Many conduct regular surveys of premiums for different types of coverage, such as auto or homeowners. These surveys can give you an idea of which companies sell insurance in your area and what the typical premiums are. Some departments tally and publicize which companies have received the most consumer complaints.

States also assist residents who can't get insurance. Since drivers must have auto insurance, every state has some mechanism to provide coverage to high-risk drivers who can't buy it on the open market. Some states have programs for

YOUR TAX DOLLARS AT WORK

STATE	TELEPHONE NUMBERS[†]
Alabama	334-241-4141
Alaska	800-467-8725/907-465-2515
Arizona	800-325-2548/602-912-4000
Arkansas	800-852-5494 /501-371-2600
California	800-927-HELP
Colorado	303-894-7490
Connecticut	800-203-3447/860-297-3800
Delaware	800-282-8611/302-739-4251
District of Columbia	202-727-8000
Florida	800-342-2762/904-922-3130
Georgia	404-656-2070
Hawaii	808-586-2790
Idaho	800-721-3272/208-334-4250
Illinois	217-782-4515/312-814-2427
Indiana	800-622-4461/317-232-2395
Iowa	515-281-5705
Kansas	800-432-2484/913-296-3071
Kentucky	502-564-6034
Louisiana	504-342-1259
Maine	800-300-5000/207-624-8475
Maryland	800-492-6116/410-333-6300
Massachusetts	617-521-7777
Michigan	517-373-0240
Minnesota	800-657-3602/612-297-7161
Mississippi	800-562-2957/601-359-3569

† 800 NUMBERS MAY BE AVAILABLE FROM IN-STATE LOCATIONS ONLY

homeowners, and increasingly, they are helping citizens obtain health insurance, whether by mandating "open enrollment" periods when private insurers have to take all comers or by setting up their own health-insurance pools. Many states also make insurance counseling and materials on medigap and long-term

| | | | PREMIUM SURVEYS AVAILABLE | | | PROGRAMS FOR THE UNINSURABLE | | | |
Automobile	Home	Term Life	Ind. Health	Medicare Supplemental	Long Term Care	Home/Renters	Ind. Health	Complaint Data	Sr. Citizen Counseling
				◆					◆
◆	◆			◆			◆	◆	◆
◆	◆						◆		
◆	◆			◆	◆		◆	◆	◆
◆	◆					◆	◆	◆	◆
◆	◆			◆	◆		◆	◆	◆
◆	◆			◆		◆	◆	◆	◆
◆	◆			◆		◆	◆	◆	◆
						◆		◆	◆
◆	◆			◆		◆	◆	◆	◆
				◆	◆	◆	◆	◆	◆
◆						◆		◆	◆
							◆		◆
◆	◆			◆		◆	◆	◆	◆
						◆	◆	◆	◆
				◆		◆	◆	◆	◆
◆	◆			◆		◆	◆		◆
◆	◆				◆	◆		◆	◆
◆	◆			◆		◆	◆		◆
◆			◆	◆	◆	◆		◆	◆
◆	◆					◆	◆		◆
				◆		◆	◆	◆	◆
◆	◆					◆	◆		◆
				◆	◆	◆	◆	◆	◆
						◆			

care available to senior citizens. If an area aging agency runs the program, the insurance department can direct you to the closest one.

In these charts, I've listed pertinent information on each state's insurance department. Don't be shy about picking up the telephone and requesting pre-

YOUR TAX DOLLARS AT WORK

STATE	TELEPHONE NUMBERS†
Missouri	800-726-7390/573-751-2640
Montana	800-332-6148/406-444-2040
Nebraska	402-471-2201
Nevada	800-992-0900 ext.7690
New Hampshire	800-852-3416/603-271-2261
New Jersey	609-292-5360
New Mexico	505-827-4548
New York	800-342-3736/212-602-0203
North Carolina	800-546-5665/919-733-7343
North Dakota	800-247-0560/701-328-2440
Ohio	800-686-1526/614-644-2658
Oklahoma	800-522-0071/405-521-3681
Oregon	503-378-4271 ext.600
Pennsylvania	717-787-2317/215-560-2630
Rhode Island	401-277-2223
South Carolina	800-768-3467/803-737-6180
South Dakota	605-773-3563
Tennessee	800-342-4029/615-741-2218
Texas	800-252-3439/512-463-6515
Utah	800-439-3805/801-538-3805
Vermont	802-828-3302
Virginia	800-552-7945/804-371-9741
Washington	800-562-6900/360-753-7300
West Virginia	800-642-9004/304-558-3386
Wisconsin	800-236-8517/608-266-9893
Wyoming	800-438-5768 /307-777-7401

† 800 NUMBERS MAY BE AVAILABLE FROM IN-STATE LOCATIONS ONLY

mium surveys or other information you may need.

One caveat: in May 1996, the Cambridge, Massachusetts–based Center for Insurance Research published a study criticizing the service that callers receive from state insurance departments. They found that

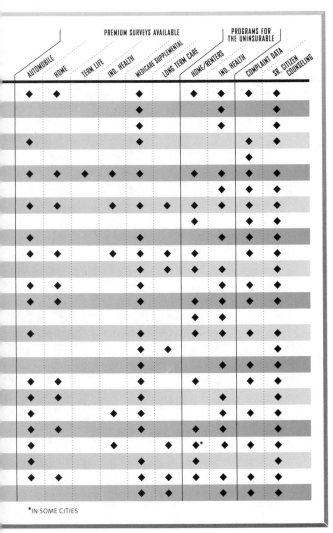

	PREMIUM SURVEYS AVAILABLE						PROGRAMS FOR THE UNINSURABLE			
AUTOMOBILE	HOME	TERM LIFE	IND. HEALTH	MEDICARE SUPPLEMENTAL	LONG TERM CARE	HOME/RENTERS	IND. HEALTH	COMPLAINT DATA	SR. CITIZEN COUNSELING
♦	♦			♦		♦	♦	♦	♦
				♦			♦		♦
				♦			♦		♦
♦				♦				♦	♦
						♦			
♦	♦	♦	♦	♦		♦	♦	♦	♦
							♦	♦	♦
♦	♦			♦	♦	♦		♦	♦
						♦		♦	♦
♦				♦				♦	♦
♦	♦		♦	♦	♦	♦		♦	♦
				♦		♦	♦	♦	♦
♦	♦			♦			♦	♦	♦
♦	♦			♦		♦	♦	♦	♦
						♦	♦		
♦				♦		♦	♦	♦	♦
				♦	♦				♦
				♦				♦	♦
♦	♦			♦		♦		♦	♦
♦	♦			♦			♦		♦
♦			♦	♦			♦	♦	♦
♦	♦			♦		♦	♦		♦
♦			♦		♦	♦*	♦	♦	♦
♦									♦
♦	♦			♦	♦	♦		♦	♦
				♦	♦		♦	♦	♦

*IN SOME CITIES

staffers answering the phones are often only marginally helpful and sometimes even dispense inaccurate information. The quality of written materials fared better in the survey, but the lesson remains: cast a skeptical eye on the advice you receive when you call.

RESOURCES

THE INSURANCE CONSUMER'S TOOL KIT

INFORMATION ON INSURANCE can be just a telephone call—or a computer keystroke—away. Below are some useful resources for consumers.

GENERAL CONSUMER RESOURCES

THE NATIONAL INSURANCE Consumer Helpline is a consumer-information telephone service sponsored by several insurance-industry trade associations. Staffers are available to answer questions on auto, home, life, and disability insurance. Call 800-942-4242, 8 AM to 8 PM E.S.T, Monday through Friday.

The following associations can also provide insurance information.

◆ The **American Association of Retired Persons (AARP)** disseminates valuable information for seniors on all types of insurance (202-434-2277).

◆ The **American Bar Association** can recommend attorneys who specialize in suing insurance companies (312-988-5000).

◆ The **Consumer Federation of America (CFA).** See page 227 for more information (202-387-6121).

◆ The **National Association of Claims Assistance Professionals (NACAP)** will recommend professional claims handlers for those filing complex health-insurance claims (800-660-0665).

AUTO INSURANCE

◆ **Consumers Union** is the parent company of *Consumer Reports* magazine. It provides comparative auto-insurance quotes, for some states, for a fee (800-807-8050).

◆ **IntelliChoice** publishes *The Complete Car Cost Guide,* listing average auto-insurance costs for models (800-227-2665).

◆ **Progressive Insurance Corp.** insures some high-risk drivers and provides comparative auto-insurance quotes (800-AUTO-PRO; 800-288-6776).

HOMEOWNERS INSURANCE

◆ Both **The American Society of Appraisers** (703-478-2228) and **The Appraisers Association of America** (212-889-5404) can help you find a qualified appraiser.

◆ **Comprehensive Loss Underwriting Exchange (CLUE)** tracks insurance claims on specific properties; you can check your CLUE report for inaccuracies. The service is free if you've been rejected or have had rates hiked because of your file; otherwise, there is an $8 fee (800-456-6004).

◆ **National Flood Insurance Program** (800-638-6620)

HEALTH INSURANCE

General Information

◆ **Medical Information Bureau (MIB).** Have you been rejected for health insurance? You can check your MIB file for inaccuracies (618-426-3660).

◆ **People's Medical Society** publishes useful information about health insurance (610-770-1670).

Managed Care

◆ **The Center for the Study of Services** ranks managed-care plans and publishes its findings. Write to *The Consumer Guide to Health Plans,* 733 15th Street, N.W., Suite 820, Washington, D.C. 20005; cost is $12 (800-475-7283).

◆ **National Committee for Quality Assurance (NCQA)** provides accreditation for managed-care companies (on-line at http://www.ncqa.org or call 800-839-6487).

◆ The August 1996 issue of *Consumer Reports* magazine rates managed-care companies.

Medicare/medigap

◆ The **Health Insurance Association of America** has useful booklets for consumers, such as *A Consumer's Guide to Medicare Supplemental Insurance* (202-824-1600).

◆ Your local **Social Security** office has a free booklet called *Your Medicare Handbook,* which describes programs.

◆ **The United Seniors Health Cooperative** publishes *How to Be An Informed Consumer of Health Insurance; 1996 Medigap Update and Medicare Summary.* Write to USHC 1996 Update, 1331 H St., N.W., #500, Washington, D.C. 20005-4706; cost is $1 for postage and handling (202-393-6222).

◆ Your local agency for the aging often has specific information about medigap policies sold in your area and may offer free advice to seniors grappling with Medicare problems.

LIFE INSURANCE

PROBABLY THE NATION'S foremost insurance consumer-advocacy group is that of the **Consumer Federation of America.** This group, formerly the independent National Insurance Consumer Organization, publishes a useful life-insurance guide, called *Taking A Bite Out of Insurance.* Write to Consumer Federation of America, 1424 16th Street, N.W., Suite 604, Washington, D.C. 20036 ($13.95; 202-387-6121). The group also provides an extremely valuable service which will analyze an existing or proposed cash-value life-insurance policy. For a $40 fee, Jim Hunt, an actuary and a former insurance commissioner of Vermont, will evaluate a policy and make recommendations on whether a policy is right for you. If you are thinking of switching one existing policy for another, the service is a must. For information on the CFA Insurance Group Life-Insurance Rate of Return Service, call 202-387-0087.

◆ **Fee for Service** (800-974-5662) and the **Life Insurance Advisers Association** (800-521-4578) can direct you to fee-only advisers.

LIFE-INSURANCE QUOTE SERVICES

THE FOLLOWING SERVICES will give you competing quotes on term life policies. The quotes are free; companies get a commission if you buy the policy through them. The only exception is Insurance Information, Inc., which doesn't sell life insurance and therefore charges $50 to provide quotes.

◆ **Direct Quote** (800-845-3853)
◆ **Insurance Information, Inc.** (800-472-5800)
◆ **InsuranceQuote Services** (800-972-1104)
◆ **QuickQuote** (800-867-2404)
◆ **Quotesmith** (800-431-1147)
◆ **Select Quote** (800-343-1985)
◆ **TermQuote** (800-444-8376)
◆ **Wholesale Insurance Network** (800-808-5810)

INSURANCE COMPANIES

BELOW ARE SOME OF THE insurance companies mentioned throughout this book.

◆ **Allstate** (local agents are listed in telephone directories)
◆ **American Express Co.** (800-535-2001)
◆ **Ameritas** (800-552-3553)
◆ **Amica** (800-242-6422)
◆ **Charles Schwab & Co.,** while not an insurer, does sell low-load life insurance (800-542-LIFE).
◆ **GEICO** (800-841-3000)

- **New York Savings Bank Life Insurance** (800-GET-SBLI)
- **Northwestern Mutual Life Insurance** (414-271-1444)
- **Provident Life and Accident Co.** (423-755-1011)
- **State Farm** (local agents listed in telephone directories)
- **20th Century** (in California and Arizona, call 800-211-SAVE)
- **UNUM Life Insurance Co. of America** (207-770-2211)
- **USAA** (800-531-8100)
- **Wholesale Insurance Network** (800-808-5810)

INSURANCE RATING AGENCIES

THE FOLLOWING FIRMS rate the financial stability of insurers. Some charge a fee for providing ratings to consumers. For further information on these companies, see page 147.

- **A.M. Best** (800-424-BEST)
- **Duff & Phelps** (312-368-3198)
- **Moody's** (212-553-0377)
- **Standard & Poor's** (212-208-1527)
- **Weiss Ratings** (800-289-9222)

ON-LINE RESOURCES

ALL YOU NEED IS TO TYPE the word "insurance" into one of the Internet search engines to turn up thousands of Web sites relating to the topic. It seems like every local insurance agency, as well as every large insurance company, has posted its own home page. Meanwhile, the Internet and the major consumer on-line services are also a good source of information about insurance.

Insurance News Network (http://www.insure.com) is an independent, on-line news service with an abundance of valuable consumer information. For example, INN carries data from state insurance departments, term-life-insurance premium surveys, and financial-health ratings on insurers from Standard & Poor's and Duff & Phelps. It takes advertising but is not an industry trade group and doesn't sell insurance.

The net site for the **National Association of Insurance Commissioners** (http://www.naic.org) can help with information on state regulation of insurance and may be linked to your own state's Web site, if one exists. Many state insurance departments have now posted home pages, providing easy access to their comparative premium surveys.

Quicken's Insure Market (http://www.insuremarket.com) site mixes advice and information with an on-line quote service and sales information for specific policies.

All of the commercial on-line services have insurance information, often in their personal finance or money section. IMHO (in my humble opinion, in on-line jargon), one of the liveliest bulletin boards concerning insurance is currently on **Prodigy** (jump: Money Talk BB, topic: insurance). It's a lively community of insurance agents, consultants, and professors who debate various issues and answer questions posted by readers. **CompuServe** has a message board much like it under its Consumer Forum. Valuable insurance information can be found on **America Online** by visiting the AARP area, the Real Life Personal Finance message board under Personal Finance, or for health insurance info, the Better Health section.

PERIODICALS

WHILE INSURANCE HASN'T BEEN as comprehensively covered by the general business press as other aspects of financial planning, several of the personal-finance publications do a fine job of reporting on insurance issues of interest to consumers.

Most notable in this category is *Consumer Reports,* which periodically rates different types of policies and surveys consumers for customer-satisfaction levels. *Bloomberg Personal, Forbes, Kiplinger's, Smart-Money, The Wall Street Journal,* and *Worth* all regularly cover the topic, while Jane Bryant Quinn's column in *Newsweek* consistently offers consumers solid advice on insurance.

One of the most respected newsletters is *The Insurance Forum,* published by Joseph Belth, an insurance professor associated with Indiana University. *The Insurance Forum* publishes financial-stability ratings of companies and covers sophisticated insurance issues, such as the demutualization of certain insurance companies. While perhaps too detailed to be of interest to most insurance consumers, Belth's newsletter is a must-read in the industry. (*The Insurance Forum,* P.O. Box 245, Ellettsville, IN 47429-0245; subscriptions are $60 per year.)

INDEX

ABOUT THE AUTHOR

Janet Bamford has specialized in personal finance reporting for over a decade. Previously with *Forbes* and *American Lawyer*, she is the author of the insurance sections of *The Consumer Reports Money Book* and contributes regularly to *Bloomberg Personal*. She has written for *Business Week, Investor's Business Daily, SmartMoney, Worth,* and *Family Business.*